PLANNING THE DEFEAT OF JAPAN:
A STUDY OF TOTAL WAR STRATEGY

Lt. Col. Henry G. Morgan, Jr.

Prepared in

The Office of the Chief of Military History
Washington 25, D.C.

Not to be reproduced in any
form without permission.

Published by Books Express Publishing
Copyright © Books Express, 2011
ISBN 978-1-78039-064-2

Books Express publications are available from all good retail and online booksellers. For publishing proposals and direct ordering please contact us at: info@books-express.com

PREFACE

The progress of the war in the Pacific and the military strategy employed by the United States against Japan were largely determined by state policy and by military plans and preparations during the preceding years of peace. As William James wrote half a century ago:

> Every up-to-date dictionary should say that "peace" and "war" mean the same thing, now in _posse_, now in _actu_. It may even reasonably be said that the intensely sharp competitive preparation for war by the nation is the real war, permanent, unceasing; and that the battles are only a sort of public verification of the mastery gained during the "peace" interval.[1]

Thus, the Pacific War was unique in this respect; but as the unfolding events of the drama pass in review, one is struck with the thought that the real options open to strategists in time of war are far fewer than he might have imagined. The growing awareness of this serious truth presses heavily on men's consciousness today and is manifested in the current desperate effort to plan _now_ to forestall if possible and otherwise to prosecute successfully the next war.

This is not to deny the direct and vital influence of the will of individuals on events after the war started; for some strong men, indeed, a few giant-sized personalities were participants in those events. The narrative of the study should make this clear enough.

---

[1] _Memories and Studies_ (1911), p. 273.

However, it is concerned not so much with the progress of battles as with major political and military decisions. With the ideas and concepts behind those decisions, and with the men who made them; in a word, with strategy. It concerns especially the strategy employed against Japan, how and to what extent it was fixed before the war began, and how and to what extent it was developed after the war began. This is an ambitious project for a study, and the effort to keep it in reasonable proportions and still say something worthwhile is explained below.

I conceive the development of this strategy to be first of all an inter-service story, secondly an inter-theater story, and thirdly an international (American and British) story. The organization of the narrative is generally chronological, but it is not intended to be a complete and definitive history of the development of Pacific strategy, much less of the Pacific War. Nevertheless, from a vast amount of information available, enough has been culled to treat at some point every one of the most important elements of Pacific strategy. Each of them was debated endlessly before and during the war, but I have endeavored to avoid repetition of ideas and arguments of the strategic planners except when they were resurrected and reused in a somewhat different context and when they led to new ideas or to new decisions. In this way I have attempted to place them in the proper perspective of time and importance.

The introduction and the first two numbered chapters are devoted to the prewar period. This is no more than a fair apportionment of space in light of the great influence of prewar plans and preparations on the development of the wartime strategy to defeat Japan. This should be clear after a reading of the section entitled "Some Major Problems of Strategy" in Chapter IV. That section is the real heart of the study. None of the problems considered there were completely new, and some of them had been considered at great length in the years before the war.

The study has literally been built around long-range planning, the subject of Chapter IV, which may partly account for both its weakness and its merit. Building both backwards and forward from this central position has provided a guide for eliminating a great deal which had only an indirect bearing on the main theme. For example, little is said about the war in Europe against Germany and Italy and almost as little about the war in the Indian Ocean and on the Continent of Asia against Japan. Even the war in the Pacific is held together by a very thin thread running through Chapters III and V. The reader who is completely unfamiliar with the complicated war in the Pacific may find these omissions an impediment to understanding. This problem, if it exists, may be partially overcome through the use of Appendices A and B, a chronology and a map of the Pacific War.

We are blessed with a wonderfully supple language, but its very flexibility can be a limitation. One slippery word in English is

"Strategy." It is a word so important to this study that the reader is entitled to some explanation of my use of it and its adjectival and adverbial derivatives. It is often used in connection with non-military activities and is not consistently applied even to the employment of armed forces. An important reason for the latter is that its meaning is relative and depends upon the position of the user. Thus, what an officer commanding a battalion, a destroyer, or a squadron sees as a problem of strategy would be seen by that same officer as a problem in minor tactics if he were a planner of the Combined Chiefs of Staff. Strategy in this study is usually viewed from the level of the national government -- the level of the Commander in Chief, the Joint Chiefs of Staff, and the two departments of the armed services. At this level, strategy, or more precisely, grand strategy, merges often with current national policy and even with more permanent national aims. The same is true at the next higher level of the Combined Chiefs of Staff and heads of government of the United States and the United Kingdom. At the Pacific Theater level, to which the reader will occasionally step down to view the war, strategy is at times almost the same as grand strategy and at times no more than a matter of tactics. At this level more appropriate phrases such as theater strategy, operational strategy, and grand tactics are used.

Webster's unabridged dictionary defines strategy as "the science and art of applying the armed strength of a belligerent to secure the objects of war." What keeps this definition from being precise is the impreciseness of "objects of war." The direction of armed forces for the attainment of political ends is guided first by national aims, national policy, and grand strategy formulated at the governmental level; then by theater strategy, operational strategy, and grand tactics formulated by the military services at the national and theater levels. The direct (tactical) application of combat power is then the responsibility of military commanders in the field. The study is concerned almost solely with the strategy and the "objects of war" determined at the national and international levels of government.

Off and on during 1958 and 1959 I was associated with Dr. Louis Morton in the preparation of the sequel volume to his <u>Strategy and Command: The First Two Years</u>, a forthcoming volume in the Pacific subseries of the UNITED STATES ARMY IN WORLD WAR II. Preparation of the sequel volume has been suspended, but I have become familiar with Dr. Morton's first volume and with much of the source material on which it is based. Moreover, two studies of mine, one on the evolution of the Long Range Plan for the Defeat of Japan and a section of another one on the formation, functioning, and relationship of the Combined Chiefs of Staff, the Joint Chiefs of Staff, and the Pacific theater commands were used freely by Dr. Morton in the final revision of his book.

This association should explain why the study was developed as it was, from the middle out. It should also explain my heavy debt to Dr.

Morton and to other authors in the Office of the Chief of Military History, Department of the Army (hereafter abbreviated OCMH). Together they have provided not only direct assistance of many kinds but, just as important, a congenial and stimulating environment as well. Dr. Stetson Conn, Chief Historian of OCMH, has read the manuscript and offered many helpful comments. I am also indebted to my military superiors -- Brigadier General James A. Norell, Chief of Military History, Lt. Colonel James C. Griffin, Executive, and Lt. Colonel William G. Bell, Acting Chief of the Histories Division for deliberately lightening my duties as Chief, Post-World War II Branch, OCMH while this study was in preparation. A number of archivists at the World War II Records Center of the National Archives as well as the ladies at the reference desk there were unfailingly helpful and friendly. Mrs. Hazel Ward, especially, gave me many research leads and spent much time in searches and much energy in bringing to me the results of those searches. Finally, I would like to thank Mrs. Eileen Blandford for combing skill and patience in typing drafts as well as the final manuscript and in the process catching a number of lapses in spelling and grammar.

But despite these debts, the study, with all its shortcomings, is my own. My colleagues may well not wish to indorse some of its conclusions, however much they may wish me well.

TABLE OF CONTENTS

	Page
PREFACE	iii

Chapter

	INTRODUCTION: THE SEEDS OF CONFLICT AND STRATEGY.	1

    Expansion in the Pacific
    The Rising Sun

I.	PRE-WAR POLICY: A TRICHOTOMY OF COMMITMENTS, MEANS, AND PLANS	9

    The Joint Board
    Developing a One-Front Strategy: Plan ORANGE
    Developing a Two-Front Strategy: Plans RED-ORANGE
       and RAINBOW

II.	PREPARING FOR COALITION WARFARE: A STRATEGY OF FRIENDLY NEUTRALITY.	34

    Military Liaison with Britain
    Some Military Views
    Pre-War Conferences
    RAINBOW 5
    Strengthening the Pacific

III.	THE FIRST TWO YEARS OF WAR: A STRATEGY OF ADJUSTMENT.	69

    Organizing for Coalition War
    Organizing the Pacific
    The Counteroffensive
    Theater Command and Strategy
    CARTWHEEL
    Starting the Central Pacific Advance

IV.	THE LONG-RANGE PLAN: COMMITMENT TO TOTAL WAR.	95

    Strategic Concepts and Nascent Plan
    The First Long-Range Plan
    The Major Strategic Factors
    Combined Decisions and Plans -- TRIDENT to QUADRANT
    The Air Plan for the Defeat of Japan
    Combined Decisions and Plans -- QUADRANT to SEXTANT

Chapter	Page

V. THE LAST TWO YEARS OF WAR: REACHING THE FINAL
DECISIONS 133

    The Theaters Agree
    The Joint Chiefs Disagree
    Speed-up in the Pacific
    Luzon versus Formosa
    Invasion Reconsidered
    Reorganizing the Pacific
    OLYMPIC -- Final Negotiations

SUMMATION: A REFLECTION AND APPRAISAL 169

    Pre-War Planning and Preparation
    Wartime Planning and Operations
    Service Differences over Strategy
    The Winning Strategy

APPENDIX 194

A. Chronology of the Pacific War

INTRODUCTION: THE SEEDS OF CONFLICT AND STRATEGY

American interest in the Pacific is as old as the Republic itself. But for one and a quarter centuries this interest was chiefly a matter of economics. Eighteenth Century merchantmen sailing out of Salem, Boston, and other Atlantic ports, returned from China with cargoes which brought a one thousand percent return on the cost of their long voyage. Later, American whalers began to range the Pacific while still other Americans were attracted to the coast of Alaska and Oregon by fish and furs. But unlike other maritime powers who were building oversea empires, the United States was simply pushing her borders out overland. America's Manifest Destiny may have had some finite limits but they were great enough to sate most expansionist ambitions.[1]

And so it was simply the pursuit of markets for trade that led Commodore Matthew C. Perry to Japan in 1853. As a result of the treaty he negotiated the next year, the credit for inducing Japan to drop her long-held policy of isolation, to open her doors to trade, and to

---

[1] The facts presented in this "Introduction" are generally well known. For specific data the following three works have been used as sources: Louis Morton, Strategy and Command: The First Two Years, MS, a forthcoming book in the Pacific subseries of the HISTORY OF THE U.S. ARMY IN WORLD WAR II, to be published by the Government Printing Office; Foster Rhea Dulles, America in the Pacific (2d ed.; Boston: Houghton Mifflin Co., 1938); and Chitoshi Yanaga, Japan Since Perry (New York: McGraw-Hill Book Co., Inc., 1949).

resume the normal activities of intercourse among nations belongs to America. The irony of this has often been remarked in recent years, for the last two great political powers to enter the political race in the Western Pacific were Japan and the United States. And it was the growing conflict of interest of these two which precipitated the greatest war ever fought in that part of the world.

Expansion in the Pacific

Some American explorers, several naval officers among them, did attempt to establish territorial claims from time to time early in the Nineteenth Century, but their acts never received official sanction. After the passage of the Guano Act of 1856, claims were made to a number of small islands, but interest waned as the valuable guano deposits were exhausted, and most of the claims were forfeited by default. A few of these claims, however, were never challenged by other nations, and the possession of such dots in the ocean as Howland, Baker, and Palmyra was fortunate when World War II came along.

The years between the Civil War and the Spanish American War were a period of great introversion for the United States. There were spiritual and physical wounds to be healed, political fences to be mended, great western lands to be settled, and new industries to develop. Consequently, the negotiations for and the consumation of the agreement to purchase Alaska and the Aleutian Islands from Russia in 1867 were practically a one-man operation on the American side and were carried out in the face of a largely apathetic or hostile public opinion. The man who managed this was Secretary of State William H. Seward, a long-time and outspoken expansionist. The economic value of the new territory was apparent within a few years but its strategic importance was little appreciated until World War II.

The early reaction to "Seward's Folly" was wide-spread ridicule and criticism. But in the same year and in the midst of this hue and cry, that determined man went quietly about arranging for the annexation of Midway Island, the scene seventy-five years later of the great naval battle which would mark the turning point of the war with Japan.

Other events and other forces, too, were in the vanguard of the great outburst of imperialism of 1898. It did not, after all, appear suddenly full-grown. The Navy was taking ever greater interest in the Pacific. Naval commanders were frequently intrusted with diplomatic missions and sometimes undertook certain actions on their own initiative.[1] Men like Perry and Admiral George E. Belknap spoke out forcefully about the need for bases; and the views of Captain Alfred Thayer Mahan, the noted writer and theorist on sea power, exerted great influence in the 1890's. In 1878 the United States secured by treaty the

---

[1] E.g., the Navy's early activities in Samoa. See Dulles, p. 103.

excellent harbor of Pago Pago in the Eastern Samoas, and in 1884 it secured an option on a base at Pearl Harbor.

It was in 1898 that United States power was carried deep into the Western Pacific in a sudden series of giant strides. During the year the long-delayed union of Hawaii with the mainland was consumated. Uninhabited Wake Island, halfway between Midway and the Marianas, was also annexed. Guam Island in the Southern Marianas, and the largest of the group, was captured from the Spanish, as was Manila in Luzon. Japan undoubtedly had held great interest in Hawaii, but the projection of American sovereignty into the Western Pacific was of even greater concern to her. Coming so close on the heels of her conflict with other Western nations in China,[1] and combined with the problems of a growing commercial competition and a growing interest in Japan in the markets and resources of Southeast Asia, it augured ill for the future.

The American conscience was not untroubled over the acquisition of the Philippines, anyway. Here was imperialism of a new order. The islands were not sparsely populated, they were not completely uncivilized, and they were not eager to become a possession of the United States. Their retention required a new rationale. The one finally adopted was a mixture of somewhat equal quantities of commercialism

---

[1] See next section of this Introduction, below.

and mysticism and a certain portion of more or less justified defense needs.[1]

In this same year of 1898 the British Government first approached the U.S. Government with the suggestion that the two cooperate in guaranteeing equal commercial rights in China.[2] Not interested at first, the next year the United States took the lead in securing agreements toward this end. This new policy of the Open Door quickly took its place alongside the Monroe Doctrine as one of the few basic elements of American foreign policy. Although Japan endorsed the policy, it was in complete disharmony with her ambitions, a fact constantly and unhappily evident for the next half century.

The capstone to the new position of the United States as a Pacific power came with the completion of the Panama Canal in 1914.

The Rising Sun

The trade treaty with the United States, signed in Japan in 1854, was followed by similar treaties with other nations. Finally awakened from her long hibernation, she took a page or two out of the book of the western powers as a guide for her own future conduct. Before long she was writing a book peculiarly her own. Between 1875 and 1880, by

---

[1] For an interesting development of a similar view see, George F. Kennan, *American Diplomacy, 1900-1950* (Chicago: University of Chicago Press, 1951), Chap. iii.

[2] Yanaga, p. 279.

largely peaceful means, she extended her sovereignty over the Kuriles, the Bonins and the Ryukyus. The Sino-Japanese War of 1894-95 gained for her Formosa, the Pescadores, and the Liaotung Peninsula. This success enhanced her prestige, increased her self-confidence, and whetted her appetite for more of the same. But her exhuberance was short-lived. Before the final peace treaty with China was signed, the Triple Intervention of Russia, Germany, and France forced Japan to retrocede Liaotung. She was stung deeply by this. Her anger rose as the intervening powers proceeded to secure concessions for themselves from China, and it was hardly mitigated by the United States' acquisitions in the Western Pacific in 1898.

During the next decade Japan prospered and grew stronger militarily. Still smarting, she nevertheless acted with restraint. For her part in suppressing the Boxer Rebellion, for example, she won the respect and even the gratitude of the Allies.

But conflict with Russia grew closer as Russian influence spread throughout Manchuria. Diplomatic relations were severed on February 6, 1904; two days later Japanese forces attacked Port Arthur; and two days later still Japan declared war.[1] In a series of costly, but stunning victories during 1904 and 1905 the Japanese Army cleared Korea, captured Port Arthur, and finally defeated the main Russian Army at

---

[1] Ibid., pp. 289, 306.

Mukden. Russia's defeat was complete after the first fleet which she sent out from the Baltic was destroyed. As a result of the Treaty of Portsmouth, Russia recognized the paramount interest of Japan in Korea, transferred her rights in the Liaotung Peninsula, ceded the southern sector of the Manchurian Railway, and ceded the southern half of Sakhalin.[1] Japan made substantial gains from the war, but the populace had been led to expect even greater gains. The result was disappointment and resentment directed toward the United States for her part in mediating the conflict.

In 1909 Japan added Korea to her Empire; and in 1914 she seized the Marshall, Caroline, and Marianas Islands from Germany and took over German property and interests in China. The offensive Twenty-one Demands, which she made of China in 1915, were withdrawn largely at the insistence of the United States.

The relations of the United States and Japan had been traditionally friendly, but by the early part of the Twentieth Century their interests were colliding in an increasing number of areas. Whereas the one had just taken up the white man's burden, the other was seeking to relieve all white men of it; whereas in the realms of both politics and economics the United States was now quite content with the status quo, Japan was quite insistent upon change.

---

[1] Ibid., pp. 313 - 14.

For the maintenance of the _status quo_ the United States was prepared to rely heavily upon words of a high morale tone. What military force she had been obliged to employ to achieve her position had been largely obscured and depreciated. After all, Admiral Dewey's mission had been to destroy the Spanish fleet, not to conquer the Philippines. And had not the Philippines been purchased for $20,000,000?

Japan drew a somewhat different lesson from her experience. She had gained much from two limited wars, both of which were initiated without warning and prosecuted with vigor.

CHAPTER I

PRE-WAR POLICY:
A TRICHOTOMY OF COMMITMENTS, MEANS, AND PLANS

The emergence of the United States as a world power in possession of a colonial empire gave new significance to her foreign policies. This was especially true of her Far Eastern policies now that American power was permanently lodged in the Philippines. At the same time and for the same reasons there were thrust upon the nation some unwonted responsibilities; and these responsibilities entailed some clearly unwanted military problems.

Foremost among the foreign policies of the United States, predating even the Monroe Doctrine and the no-alliance policy, was the traditional insistence upon the freedom of the seas. And now, a perfect corollary and complement to it, came the Open Door of China policy. The basic objective of the latter was to assure equal opportunities for exploiting the markets of China. But the real meaning was often obfuscated by a more euphemistic interpretation: the guaranteeing of the sovereignty and of the territorial integrity of China. In the beginning this latter interpretation was valid just to the extent that it strengthened the first, but through the years its emotional appeal grew stronger and spread wider throughout the United States.[1]

Beyond these two, the policies of the United States in the Far East were none too clear. For example, the ultimate aim of the Philippines was unknown, although there was clearly no intention of giving them up to another colonial power.[2] Theodore Roosevelt made this quite clear during his presidency, and there apparently was never any change in this policy.

The Joint Board

Upholding these policies by force was primarily, though not exclusively, a naval problem. The defense of the insular possessions was also chiefly a naval problem except in the Philippines, where substantial army forces were needed. Thus, for the first time, the Army and the Navy were faced with a continuing need for joint strategic planning and for close coordination of operations. To satisfy these needs the Joint Army and Navy Board was organized by the two service

---

[1] A good resume of Japanese-American relations and a good example of this obfuscation can be found in a draft of a proposed message to Congress by the President, dated 29 November 1941. It was prepared by officers of the War, State, and Navy Departments and can be found in U.S. Congress, Joint Committee on the Investigation of the Pearl Harbor Attack, 79th Cong., 2d Sess., 1946, Exhibit No. 19. Hereafter cited as Pearl Harbor Hearings.

[2] See the arguments of Senator Albert J. Beveridge, for example, quoted and commented on by Dulles, America in the Pacific, p. 262.

secretaries in 1903.[1] Presided over during the first years by the hero of Manila Bay, Admiral Dewey, the Board was composed of eight members, four senior officers from each of the two services. It performed extremely valuable services through the years, especially between the two World Wars, but its usefulness in the early years depended heavily upon the interest of the President and his support of its work. Its mission was modest and purely advisory. In 1919 its organization was strengthened somewhat by reducing its membership to six, the Chief of Staff and Chief of Naval Operations, their senior assistants, and the Chiefs of their War Plans Divisions. At the same time a permanent Joint Planning Committee was established.

In 1904 the Joint Board undertook the development of a number of war plans, each for fighting a war with one enemy. A color code name was assigned each plan -- RED for Great Britain, ORANGE for Japan, etc. After a plan was approved by both service secretaries, each service

---

[1] Most Joint Board files through October 1938 have recently been released by the Joint Chiefs of Staff to the National Archives. Good secondary sources on which I have drawn are Louis Morton, Strategy and Command; Maurice Matloff and Edwin M. Snell, Strategic Planning for Coalition Warfare, 1941-1942 (Washington: U.S. Government Printing Office, 1953), esp. parts of Chap. i; Mark Watson, Chief of Staff: Prewar Plans and Preparations (Washington: U.S. Government Printing Office, 1950), pp. 79,- 81, 97; National Archives Publication No. 51 - 8, Federal Records of World War II, Vol. II: Military Agencies (Washington: U.S. Government Printing Office), p. 37; Ray S. Cline, Washington Command Post: The Operations Division (Washington: U.S. Government Printing Office, 1951), pp. 44 - 47.

prepared a detailed implementing plan of operations for its forces. Most early plans were little more than theoretical exercises based on remotely possible but hardly probable causes and areas of conflict. From the start, however, Plan ORANGE was an exception. The effort to keep it current and realistic was destined to have a long history.

Developing a One-Front Strategy: Plan ORANGE[1]

That history really began in 1907. Fifty years of good relations between the United States and Japan had come to an abrupt end with the termination of the Russo-Japanese War in 1905. Interests of the two nations began to clash in the Far East and the future held only prospects of greater conflict. The segregation order of the San Francisco School Board in 1906 increased the tension, and talk of war was widespread. When President Theodore Roosevelt sought the advice of the Joint Board in the spring of 1907, the Board recommended that the Army and Navy forces in the Philippines be deployed for defense and that the Fleet be sent to Manila. If Japan attacked, the initially greater Japanese strength would require American forces to remain on the defense until reinforcements arrived, said the military chiefs and

---

[1] For this section I have drawn heavily on Morton, *Strategy and Command*, Chap. ii. A slightly expanded version of his Chap. ii, and the most complete account of the development of *Plan ORANGE* in print, can be found in his "War Plan ORANGE: Evolution of a Strategy," *World Politics*, XI (January 1959), 221 - 250.

their advisers. As it turned out, the disparity between American and Japanese strength in the Far East was never reduced but grew gradually through the years until, to the Army planners at least, it became clear that a defense could not be sustained until the arrival of reinforcements. Nevertheless, this early assumption that the Philippine garrison would attempt to hold out until reinforcements arrived became the basis of all future ORANGE planning.

The question of whether and where to establish an advance naval base in the Pacific often absorbed the thoughts of the joint military planners before World War I. The Army preferred Luzon, but the Navy preferred Hawaii and won its case in 1908. It was then agreed that a secondary base would be established in the Philippines. Again there was a disagreement. For ease of defense and for other reasons the Army wanted the base located in Manila Bay; the Navy preferred Subic Bay to the west of Bataan. The Army won its case here, but the base at Cavite on the southeastern shore of Manila Bay was never developed sufficiently to support a major fleet. Guam, too, was a desirable site for a naval base. The Navy, in fact, became convinced that it was better than Manila, but its development never got very far and had to stop altogether after the Five Power Naval Treaty of 1922 was signed.

After World War I the League of Nations mandated the formerly German Marianas, Carolines, and Marshalls to Japan. These islands lay squarely athwart the line of communications from the Philippines back to Hawaii and the West Coast. This development enormously complicated the problem of defending the Philippines and invalidated completely the former estimates of three to four months of time required for the Fleet to get reinforcements to Luzon. Now it would be a slow process of moving through the Mandated Islands, establishing bases along the way. Following this development, the Treaty of 1922 prohibited an improvement in the defense of Guam and the Philippines, making certain that the defenders of Manila Bay could not hold out long enough. This tragic truth was not always recognized thereafter except by those who were faced directly with its consequences -- the Army commanders in the field and the Army planners in Washington.[1]

Nevertheless, Army and Navy leaders were acutely aware of the growing conflict of interest between Japan and the United States in the Far East and of the indisposition of either to give way.[2] There was a constant urgency, therefore, to keep Plan ORANGE up to date in light of the latest situation and the prospects for the future. Moreover, in the early nineteen twenties, General Leonard Wood was Governor-General of the Philippines. He was a former Army Chief of Staff, quite

---

[1] The Navy sometimes agreed. See e.g., the opinion of then Capt. H. E. Yarnell, USN, a senior Navy planner, and of Adm. Sims of the Naval War College, recognizing the fallacy of the ORANGE Plan estimate. Cited by Morton, Chap. ii, pp. 8 and 10.

[2] Preliminary Estimate of the Situation, War Plan ORANGE, 3 Dec 21, Cited by Morton, Chap. ii, p. 12.

familiar with Plan ORANGE. He had many influential friends in Washington, he was articulate, and he was not content to see the defenders of the Philippines sacrificed in a hopeless task.

Finally, in September 1924, a new ORANGE Plan was approved. It represented many months of work, but in the end it "was really more a statement of hopes than a realistic appraisal of what could be done." Neither the Army nor the Navy were capable of carrying it out. It called for the immediate dispatch of 50,000 troops from the West Coast and for the establishment at the earliest possible date of American sea power in the Western Pacific "in strength superior to that of Japan." Offensive operations by naval and air forces would then be diverted toward the isolation of Japan and the crippling of her economic life. If this did not force her surrender, "such further action as may be required" would be taken.[1]

After occasional minor revisions of the plan, a completely new plan was approved in April 1928. During its preparation the planners split into two groups, one proposing a continuation of the offensive strategy and the other proposing a defensive strategy, holding the main naval forces east of Hawaii. The Joint Board supported the advocates of an offensive strategy and directed the preparation of a plan in accord with it. But in the course of the debates, arguments had been used which would be used again more

---
[1] Ibid., pp. 16 - 19.

effectively.[1]

One of the most persistent advocates of a defensive strategy was Brigadier General Stanley D. Embick. As a Captain in 1907 he had helped plan the defenses of Manila Bay. As a Colonel and Washington planner after World War I he had protested against the ORANGE Plan. In 1933, as a Brigadier General and commander of the island fortress of Corregidor in the mouth of Manila Bay, he called the plan to dispatch the fleet to the Philippines "literally an act of madness." He maintained that unless the American people were willing to bear the cost of greatly increasing the defenses of the Philippines -- this in the midst of the depression -- the only correct course was to withdraw behind the natural "strategic peacetime frontier in the Pacific," the line Alaska-Oahu-Panama.[2] Back in Washington as chief of the Army's War Plans Division, General Embick again advocated a defensive strategy which would make the United States invulnerable to attack and which would permit her

---

[1] Terming the movement to the Philippines an offensive is a paradox which can be confusing. Earlier in the century it would have been nothing more than a reinforcement of the defense of the Philippines. But it will be remembered that long before World War I it was decided to base the battle fleet at Pearl Harbor. This left only the Asiatic Fleet in the Far East. It was based in China and had limited combat power beyond that required to protect American shipping from Chinese river and coastal pirates. (See Samuel Eliot Morison, _The Rising Sun in the Pacific, 1931 - April 1942_ (Boston: Little, Brown and Co., 1948), pp. 28 - 29, 58.) After Japan received her Pacific Mandates the U.S. was faced with the prospect of a long and difficult _offensive_ to reach the Philippines, no matter how long the _local_ defense in the islands was maintained.

[2] Memo, Brig Gen S. D. Embick for CG Phil Dept, 19 Apr 33, sub: Mil Policy of U.S. in Phil Is, copy in OCMH files.

military and naval forces to operate "in such a manner that /would/ promise success instead of national disaster."[1]

Revision of the plan in 1936 reduced the Army's mission from the task of holding the Manila Bay area to simply holding the entrance to the Bay, i.e. Corregidor and three smaller island fortresses. For the first time the plan was silent regarding reinforcements.

1936 also was the year that Japan joined Germany in the Anti-Comintern Pact. The next year full scale war broke out between Japan and China -- the China Incident. In November, 1937, the Joint Board directed its Planning Committee to prepare a new ORANGE Plan which would provide for "a position of readiness." The planners were then to explore the various courses of action open to the United States after a secure defensive posture had been assumed. The army planners, reading their directive literally, were unwilling to consider the second task until all vital areas in the Western Hemisphere were secured. As much concerned with the European Axis Powers as with Japan, they saw the first task as a major and time-consuming one. But long before the Army would be satisfied with the state of Hemisphere security, the Navy would be prepared to strike out westward from Hawaii. The navy planners considered it reasonable to assume that if Germany and Italy assisted Japan, the United States could also expect outside assistance. The exact nature of that

---

[1] App. A to memo initialed S.D.E., 2 Dec 35, sub: Mil Aspects of . . . Retention of U.S. of . . . Phil Is, quoted by Morton, Chap. ii, p. 33.

assistance could not be predicted, they admitted, but the Navy promptly sent Captain Royal E. Ingersoll off to London to discuss the problem with the British.[1] Anyway, insisted the naval officers of the Joint Planning Committee, a joint war plan had to aim at the defeat of the enemy if it were to be a realistic guide for the services.[2]

In an attempt to reconcile these differences, a new directive was issued at the suggestion of Admiral William D. Leahy, Chief of Naval Operations. This time the planners were to prepare a plan whose basic objective would be the defeat of Japan but which would provide first for "an initial temporary position in readiness." But the accumulated and even growing differences between the Army and the Navy-held concepts were virtually irreconcilable. After weeks of trying but failing to reach agreement, the Joint Board gave the task to the chiefs of the two services' War Plans Divisions, General Embick and Admiral Richardson. Within a month they had an agreed plan which they submitted on 18 February 1938. The Navy preserved its concept of an advance through the Mandates without committing itself to an estimated time required for the advance. The Army won recognition of the primary importance of the "strategic triangle" in the defense of the United States. The Army again agreed to accept the mission of defending Manila Bay, but the failure to

---

[1] Infra, p.   .
[2] Morton, Chap. ii, pp. 35 - 37.

provide for reinforcement was a silent admission that the Philippine garrison faced eventual destruction.

As in every ORANGE Plan since the Russo-Japanese War, war with Japan was expected to begin with a surprise attack. This was to be the last revision of Plan ORANGE, for events were overtaking its assumptions, requiring quite a new approach to planning.

Through the years, the ORANGE Plan had been picked up for restudy and revision many times. Each time, the difference between the Army and Navy concepts resulted in unsatisfactory compromises, compromises which were very largely a reflection of the American commitment to defend its Pacific outposts and at the same time an unwillingness to provide means for their defense.[1] The Army saw as its mission the defense of the continental United States. Early in any war it would hardly have the forces necessary for this task. Only after the requirements of this primary task were satisfied was it willing to add to the local defenses of the Philippines or to undertake an offensive anywhere. Defense of what came to be called the strategic triangle -- Panama, Oahu, and Alaska -- had first call on the Army's overseas strength.

---

[1] This ambivalence of American policy is pointed out often and clearly by Morton in *Strategy and Command*, esp. in Chap. ii. The Army deplored the situation but seemed to despair of rectifying it. In a Report of the Survey of the Military Establishment by the War Department General Staff, 1 Nov 29, Army planners said that "a study of the military history of the United States shows that each of its conflicts has at the beginning found it in a state of unpreparedness for the crisis. This condition has eventuated in some cases in humiliating and disastrous reverses in the earlier stages of the wars." See p. 163. More about this remarkable document in my Bibliographic Note. Hereafter cited as *WD 1929 Survey*.

Anyway, it was the southeastern flank which concerned the Army most. A lodgement on the West Coast by an aggressive power from across the Pacific would be extremely difficult and was therefore most unlikely. The Atlantic was another matter. A powerful threat from across the Atlantic was bound to be of much greater concern to the Army, for it always considered its supreme <u>raison d'etre</u> the discouraging or repelling of any invasion.

The Navy could not agree to holding the great and growing Pacific Fleet down to the task of patrolling the strategic triangle with only an occasional foray into enemy waters. American strategy, said the Navy, must aim at the defeat of the enemy. In the Pacific this could be done by moving westward through the mandated islands and establishing "at the earliest practicable date U.S. naval power in the Western Pacific in strength superior to that of ORANGE and /operating/ offensively in that area."[1] Although the Navy wanted the Army's agreement to this strategy and wanted a greater commitment of Army forces to it, it did not agree with the Army's fear that very great Army strength would be necessary to make such a strategy successful.

Developing a Two Front Strategy: Plans RED-ORANGE and RAINBOW

The growing strength and aggressiveness of the European Fascist countries, their expanding influence in Latin America, and their

---

[1] Ltr, JPC to JB, 27 Dec 37, sub: Joint War Plan ORANGE, cited by Morton, <u>Strategy and Command</u>, Chap. ii, p. 38.

increasing ties of friendship with Japan excited more and more in American military planners a fear that the United States would be faced someday with a multiple-front war. Fear of this possibility was implicit in the Army's insistence that the 1938 version of Plan ORANGE provide first for assuming a defensive "position of readiness" within the strategic triangle, prepared for any unexpected development, before naval forces struck out in their offensive drive to the west.

Study of the problems of a two ocean war had begun as early as 1923. This arose from the Joint Planners' consideration of a RED-ORANGE war, that is, a war against a British-Japanese Alliance.[1] Even in the beginning the planners felt that such an alliance was unlikely. Nevertheless, the members of the Joint Board felt compelled to study such a possibility, and work on it continued occasionally until about 1935. In the course of it certain concepts were evolved which became virtual principles. The planners concluded that the continental United States and its vital interests in the Western Hemisphere were not vulnerable to attack from the Atlantic. Since the United States would not have the strength to undertake strategic offensives on both fronts against such powerful allies, the best course would be "to concentrate on obtaining a favorable decision" first in the Atlantic while conducting a strategic defense against

---

[1] Comments on RED-ORANGE are based entirely on Morton, Chap. ii, pp. 20 - 24. His is, I believe, the only published account of the plan.

Japan. The principal theaters of operations, therefore, would be to the Western North Atlantic and Caribbean areas for the Navy and the British possessions in North America for the Army.

No RED-ORANGE plan was ever approved, but study of the problems inherent in such a war provided valuable experience. The influence of this experience was reflected in the concepts and arguments which the planners brought to their contemporaneous planning for ORANGE. Moreover, the same concepts and arguments were carried over directly into the planning for the RAINBOW plans.

While the probability of a RED-ORANGE war was being reduced to zero, the possibilities of a similar two ocean war against a different coalition of enemies grew greater.[1] Accordingly, in November 1938, the Joint Board directed their planners to determine and evaluate the various courses of action open to the United States in the event of a simultaneous violation of the Monroe Doctrine by Germany or Italy and aggression against the United States' interests in the Pacific by Japan. The planners plunged into their task with energy and imagination.[2] For nearly six months they analyzed the problems

---

[1] On 25 October 1936, Hitler established the Rome-Berlin Axis with Mussolini and one month later signed with Japan, the Anti-Comintern Pact. These two bi-lateral accords were the start of formal collaboration among the aggressor nations. Less formal and less open collaboration had started before; thereafter it increased. The Tripartite Pact was finally signed in September 1940. See Cordell Hull, *Memoirs* (New York: The MacMillan Co., 1948), I, 488 - 89.

[2] A number of books in the series UNITED STATES ARMY IN WORLD WAR II, written by authors of OCMH, treat certain aspects of RAINBOW planning. Again I rely heavily on Dr. Morton, this time his Chap. iii of *Strategy and Command.* His account accords closely with my own interpretation of events and strategic questions, based on my fairly extensive readings in primary and other secondary sources. Mark

inherent in such a development, considered various courses of action open, and attempted to trace the consequences which would flow from each course of action. The result was a strategic study which the Joint Board found remarkably sound and comprehensive.

The planners concluded that Japan would continue to expand into China and elsewhere in Southeast Asia, peacefully if possible, by force if necessary, even at the risk of war with the Western Powers. In fact she might deliberately precipitate such a war by a surprise attack against the Fleet. Whether or not such action were in concert with moves by Germany and Italy, the United States must expect to lose all of its possessions west of 180° longitude in short order. If, in the meantime, the European Axis were contained by Britain and France, the United States could eventually undertake a counter-offensive in the Pacific, moving back to the Philippines or to the coast of China in the manner provided for in the Plan ORANGE. Four possible routes of advance had long been established in naval studies. They were via (1) the Aleutians; (2) Pearl Harbor-Midway-Luzon; (3) the Marshalls-Carolines-Marianas-Yap-Peliliu; or (4) Samoa-New Guinea-Mindanao. A combination of (2) and (3) seemed to hold the greatest promise of success. Although they did not plan to reinforce the Philippines, the planners realized that "emotionalized" public opinion might demand otherwise.

Watson, Chief of Staff: Prewar Plans and Preparations (Washington: U.S. Government Printing Office, 1950), pp. 97 - 101, 103 - 04 covers much of the same ground as does Matloff and Snell, Strategic Planning, 1941-1942, Chaps. i - iv.

Germany and Italy, the Committee concluded, would not take overt action in the Western Hemisphere unless they were assured that Britain and France would not intervene. The European democracies were not likely to acquiesce voluntarily, but if they should first be defeated, the Hemisphere would lie exposed. The United States thus had a great stake in their security, a fact which would be painfully clear the next spring when France lay prostrate and England was desperate.

The Axis Powers, especially Germany, enjoyed considerable prestige in some areas of Latin America. An Axis-supported revolution in one or more countries was a quite reasonable possibility and might well be the first aggressive movement into the Hemisphere. Converted into satellites, they would continue a grave threat to the security of the United States.[1] Therefore, said the Planners, the critical area was in the Atlantic, not in the Pacific.

An overt act by the Axis in the Western Hemisphere depended not only upon the neutrality or importance of France and England but also upon a full-scale American commitment in the Far East. A minimum defensive deployment in the Pacific would leave sufficient strength, the planners thought, to deter overt aggression from the Atlantic.

The Army used an interesting argument in support of its usual objections to heavy commitments in the Western Pacific. Army planners

---

[1] Matloff and Snell, *Strategic Planning, 1941-1942*, p. 5. The State Department was greatly concerned by this possibility also. Later, the French government was to play on these fears in their plea for more military assistance from the U.S. See Cordell Hull, *Memoirs*, pp. 495 - 97, 766 - 69.

soberly averred that the loss of Guam and the Philippines could no longer officially be considered as destructive of the country's vital interest. Had the American people and American government considered otherwise, they would never have so completely undermined, by a succession of acts, the possibility of a successful defense of these possessions; they would not have put those possessions in pawn to the already tarnished good faith of Japan by approving the treaty of 1922; they would not have refused to fortify and garrison those islands after Japan denounced the treaty in 1934; and, finally, they would not have passed the Philippine Independence Act. Yet the planners foresaw the possibility that, too late, public opinion would demand that the Western Pacific Islands be defended.[1]

---

[1] Watson, Prewar Plans and Preparations, p. 98. This attitude of the Army, especially in the years immediately preceding World War II, has often been misinterpreted. For example, even Langer and Gleason, in speaking of the defeat in Congress in February 1939 of a bill to provide $5,000,000 for harbor facilities for Guam, partly excuse Congress by saying that not only did the President and Secretary of State oppose the bill but that the Army also opposed any commitment to major operations in the Western Pacific. See William L. Langer and S. Everett Gleason, The Challenge to Isolation, 1937-1940 (New York: Harper and Brothers, 1952), pp. 149 - 50. What they seemed to overlook was the Army's long history of pleading for adequate defenses in the Western Pacific or none at all. Inadequate defenses were a waste of lives and treasure and constituted a needless provocation to potential enemies. See, e.g. WD 1929 Survey, p. 65, which called for strengthening the Pacific outposts or withdrawal of the garrisons.

Even close students of Army history of World War II can make the same mistake. See, e.g. Matloff and Snell, Strategic Planning, 1941-1942, the first par., p. 63, and the first sentence of the subsection entitled The B-17 and Defense of the Philippines, p. 69. On the other hand Mark Watson, pp. 36 - 38, believes that the psychological effect of Congress' constant refusal to provide adequate funds for defense had eventually led Army spokesmen to asking only for what they thought they might get and not what they thought they needed.

Given the assumptions laid down in the Joint Board directive to the Planning Committee, there were four broad strategies possible, and the Committee considered each one. They were (1) defense in both oceans; (2) defense in the Pacific, offense in the Atlantic; (3) defense in the Atlantic, offense in the Pacific; and (4) offense in both oceans.[1] Number four was eliminated early as being clearly beyond the capability of the United States alone, certainly without a long period of build-up of her military strength. This left just three basic strategies to consider.

The Army was not satisfied even with number three. It had only reluctantly agreed in the last ORANGE Plan to such an advance even without an aggressive enemy in the Atlantic. The Army Planners' objections ran something like this: (1) It had already been admitted that American garrisons in the Western Pacific could not hold out until relieved; (2) the offensive would be enormously difficult, requiring far greater Army resources than the Navy recognized;[2] (3) the offensive would require placing maximum strength in the Pacific, leaving the minimum strength to defend the most vulnerable flank; (4) such an advance did "not properly come within the scope of hemisphere defense";[3] and (5) the recovery of the Western Pacific was

---

[1] In their study the planners did not organize their thoughts and arguments in precisely this manner. I present it this way simply for the sake of clarity and brevity. I believe that it represents a kind of summary with which they would agree.

[2] See this opinion expressed by Brig Gen George V. Strong, Chief of Army WPD in Memo to Chief of Staff, 2 May 39, in WPD 4175-1.

[3] Ibid.

not vital in the security of the Western Hemisphere.

But the Navy planners, while readily agreeing that the Atlantic was the most critical area, would not as readily give up their plans for an offensive in the Pacific. Having first stabilized the situation in both oceans by defensive operations the Navy felt that it might then find the strength to begin its movement to the Western Pacific. At least it was too early to drop this possibility altogether, for public opinion might demand such a strategy.[1]

By this time, however, the planners had concluded that the assumptions set forth in their directive were too restrictive. Chances were good that they would face aggression from the start in the company of allies. The other two major democracies (France and England) had as great a stake as the United States in the maintenance of the status quo. In fact, any overt aggression by the Axis was likely to affect them first. The three basic strategies, therefore, became six when considered as being carried out first with and then without allies. But number one, a defense in both oceans, would not be

---

[1] This probably was the meaning of Admiral Stark's words eighteen months later. After Gen. Marshall protested against the Navy's proceeding unilaterally in developing their implementing plans for RAINBOW 3, Adm Stark replied: "Should we become engaged in the war described in the Rainbow 3, it will not be through my doings, but because those in higher authority have decided that it is to our best national interest to accept such a war." Memo, CNO for CofS, 29 Nov 40, sub: Joint Basic War Plans, Rainbows 3 and 5, WPD 4175-15.

Although I cannot document it, it seems reasonable that the Navy had another argument, viz., that without help from the European democracies and possession of European bases, it might be a long time, if ever, before the U.S. could conduct an all-out offensive against Germany and Italy; but long before that the Atlantic flank could be made reasonably secure, leaving sufficient strength for an all-out offensive against Japan.

necessary if the United States had powerful allies. This reduced to five the general sets of circumstances under which a two ocean war would most likely be fought. The Joint Planning Committee, therefore, recommended that five basic war plans be developed to cover each set of circumstances.

The descriptive code word RAINBOW was chosen for these plans for a war against several enemies, distinguishing them from the single-color, single-enemy war plans. The primary mission of the Army and Navy in each case was the security of the United States and her sea-borne trade. In practical and geographical terms, this was virtually the same thing as saying the protection of the Western Hemisphere.[1] In each, the enemies were Germany, Italy and Japan. In two of them the U.S. would be allied to France and England, and in the other three, she would fight alone or without major allies.[2]

---

[1] Different definitions were given "the Western Hemisphere" from time to time "for planning purposes." In the Atlantic the boundary usually ran along the 30° west line of longitude, including all of Greenland but none of Iceland. In the Pacific it usually included the Aleutians as far west as Unalaska, Hawaii, and the off-shore islands of Latin America. American Samoa was often included, and, on occasion, even Guam. It was sometimes considered as extending from pole to pole, but the practical southern limit was Tierra del Fuego. Antarctica and its off-shore islands were of minor strategic importance before World War II. See Stetson Conn and Byron Fairchild, *Framework of Hemisphere Defense*, to be published by the Government Printing Office, pp. 3, 5, 9, 46, 99.

[2] The planners had not overlooked the possibility of the belligerency of Spain (probably on the side of the Axis) and Russia (possibly on the side of the democracies) but their roles and effectiveness depended upon a great many imponderables.

The purpose, general situation, major assumptions, and the broad strategy to be employed in each plan can be summarized as follows:

RAINBOW No. 1. This, the basic and most conservative plan, would provide for a defense of the Western Hemisphere as far south as 10° south latitude. This would include the Brazilian and Peruvian bulges, that is, about half the land mass of South America. The requirements of this plan were the sine qua non of all other plans. The U.S. would have no major allies.

RAINBOW No. 2. This plan would provide for the projection of U.S. military power into the far Pacific, there to uphold the interests of the democratic powers, while British and French forces would keep Germany and Italy fully engaged in Europe and Africa.

RAINBOW No. 3. In this, the least conservative plan, the United States, alone, would undertake to secure the Western Hemisphere, as in Plan No. 1, and then to move out from Hawaii to secure the control of the Western Pacific.

RAINBOW No. 4. This plan could be described as a less conservative Plan No. 1. Defense of the Hemisphere, would be extended to the southern part of South America or to the Eastern Atlantic.[1] This would involve a more active defense, or what might be described as a limited offense in the Atlantic.

---

[1] Like "Western Hemisphere," "Eastern Atlantic" was not a precise term. It included areas at least as far as the Azores and Cape Verde Islands and often included coastal areas of Africa (Dakar, e.g.,) and Europe (the Iberian Peninsula, e.g.).

RAINBOW No. 5. This plan would provide for a defense in the Pacific while major offensive operations, in concert with the French and British, were undertaken against Germany and Italy.

The Joint Board approved this proposal on 30 June 1939.[1] Joint Basic War Plans -- Rainbow 1, 2, 3, 4, and 5 would be developed in that order of priority.[2]

The infinite and inter-related changes in international relations during the next few months and years could not be predicted by mortal men, but the stated bases (each basis stating the general power alignments and the general strategy to be employed by the United States) of the five proposed RAINBOW Plans were so sound that all subsequent pre-war planning could be encompassed within the framework of their general terms. In fact the developing world situation was such that the priority for developing the RAINBOW Plans remained unchanged except temporarily. The completion of one plan and the beginning of the next was timed about right to meet new circumstances and to satisfy the needs of the moment.[3]

---

[1] Morton, Chap. iii, p. 7.

[2] The reader is cautioned that secondary sources do not always clearly distinguish as I do between the Joint Basic War Plans -- RAINBOW and the corresponding plans of the services and of the field and fleet commands which implemented and supported the joint plans.

[3] Lt Gen Hugh A. Drum, CG First Army complimented the planners, saying that the plans provided "progressive steps in reaching a major effort," starting with armed neutrality and ending with preparation for overseas expeditions if the situation should warrant it. His memo to ACCS WPD, 21 Jun 39, sub: Draft Copies of Rainbow Plans, WPD 4175-11.

Preparation of Joint RAINBOW No. 1 was undertaken immediately in the spring of 1939. It was completed in August and approved by the President in October.[1]

Joint RAINBOW No. 2 was then taken up. A number of possible initial moves were open to the Japanese and each had to be considered carefully. The planners thought that the most likely was toward Hong Kong and the coast of Indo-China (Comranh Bay) rather than Malaysia.[2] In that event, there was a strong sentiment among the Army planners for moving quickly into the Netherlands East Indies via the Southwest Pacific route, avoiding the slow step-by-step process through the Mandates as the ORANGE Plans provided. The Allies would then drive the Japanese out of the Indies, and, in the peace treaty, force them to evacuate their other southern conquests (including, presumably, the Philippines and Guam.)

Completion of this plan required the close collaboration of the colonial powers and carried explosive political implications. The U.S. and British Navies had been collaborating for some time, but the idea of sending Army forces to protect Europe's colonies was quite another matter. The planners recommended that the U.S.

---

[1] President Roosevelt began to take a more direct interest in military planning at about this time. On 5 July he placed the Joint Board under his immediate supervision. Also during this period there was a change in the high command. Admiral Harold S. Stark succeeded Admiral Leahy as Chief of Naval Operations and General George C. Marshall succeeded General Malin Craig as Chief of Staff.

[2] Defined as including "the Philippines, the Malay States, the Straits Settlements, Borneo, and the Netherlands East Indies." - Section II, par 5 of the Joint Army and Navy Basic War Plan -- RAINBOW No. 5, Pearl Harbor Hearings, Exhibit N. 129.

Government propose that conversations be held with the British, French, and Dutch authorities. Until then they had gone about as far as they could with the plan by April 1940.[1]

Work was underway on Joint RAINBOW No. 3 when events in Europe seemed to overtake it in May. It was quickly suspended in favor of No. 4. Joint RAINBOW No. 3 was never completed, but the Navy continued work on their plan for several months.[2]

Since RAINBOW Nos. 2 and 3 both provided for initial offensives in the Pacific they were finally cancelled by the Joint Board on 6 August 1941. By then the United States was firmly committed to a Europe-first strategy.[3]

The Germans began their blitzkrieg in the west on 10 May 1940. In late May and early June 1940, working with a great sense of urgency, the joint planners completed RAINBOW 4.[4] Even if England fell, the United States probably now had strength enough to go beyond RAINBOW 1. A few months later Britain had defeated Germany's air offensive, and a few months later still pressure on her home territory was further relieved when Hitler turned his armies to the east against Russia.

---

[1] Matloff and Snell, pp. 9 - 10.

[2] Infra, p.

[3] Watson, p..104.

[4] It was approved by the President on 14 Aug 40. Ltr, Lt Col W. P. Scobey to SGS, WO, sub: Presidential Approval of Joint Board Paper, 16 Aug 40, in WPD 4175-12.

Still, another year would pass before the U.S. military leaders felt confident enough to cancel RAINBOW 1 and 4. This was done on 4 May 1942.[1]

---

[1] Watson, p. 104.

CHAPTER II

PREPARING FOR COALITION WARFARE: A STRATEGY OF FRIENDLY NEUTRALITY

Military Liaison with Britain

It is ironic that an important incident in late 1937 which was really a part of the last effort toward developing a one-front war strategy, marked, at the same time, the beginning of formal collaboration between the United States and the United Kingdom in preparation for a global, multi-front war. This incident was the mission of Captain Royal E. Ingersoll to London. The instigation of this mission is not perfectly clear from the record, but it may be readily inferred. Two years later, Admiral Richardson wrote to Admiral Stark that

> when the Chinese incident started /September 1937/ and on every opportunity until I left the job as assistant C.N.O. I used to say to Leahy, Be sure to impress on the /President/ that we do not want to /be/ drawn into this unless we have others so bound to us that they cannot leave us in a lurch.
>
> There is a possibility that this constant repetition had something to do with the trip of Ingersoll.[1]

It will be remembered that in the process of revising Plan ORANGE for the last time beginning in November 1937, the Army was insistent that an advance in the Pacific should not be made at the expense of leaving the Hemisphere exposed. The Navy members of the Joint Planning Committee were quick to acknowledge the greater vulnerability of the Atlantic flank, but they were less concerned than the Army members

---

[1] Letter to Stark, 26 Jan 40, *Pearl Harbor Hearings*, Exhibit 9.

over the immediate threat to that flank. The heirs of Alfred Thayer Mahan had perhaps a keener appreciation of the role of the British Fleet in protecting the Atlantic flank of America than did their Army associates. Throughout their careers, U.S. Naval officers were kept constantly aware of the presence, the capabilities, and the mission (in general terms) of the Royal Navy. In the Far East, especially, and in foreign ports throughout the world, British and American naval officers became personally acquainted. And so it was quite natural for the navy planners to suggest that if, in a war with Japan, the Axis powers should act in concert, it was likely that the United States, too, would not fight alone.

The Navies Confer

It was in the midst of these discussions that Captain Ingersoll, Director of the Navy's War Plans Division was sent in late December 1937 to London to converse with his counterpart in the Admiralty, then Captain Tom Phillips. Ingersoll received his instructions personally from President Roosevelt as well as from Admiral Leahy. He later said of his assignment that

> the primary mission was to investigate and to talk with the British Admiralty officials as to what we could do if the United States and /England/ were to find themselves at war with Japan in the Pacific /and to determine/ what arrangements it would be necessary to make in regard to command relationships, in regard to communications with each other, of establishing liaison officers, and preparing certain codes and ciphers, and so forth. [1]

---

[1] In testimony before the Joint Committee of Congress investigating the Pearl Harbor attack, Pearl Harbor Hearings, pp. 4273 - 77.

No official agreements were reached; indeed, Ingersoll was not authorized to make commitments; but a fruitful beginning was made in the discussion of essentially technical problems, discussions which would continue on about the same level of formality for three years until the American-British conversations in Washington and Singapore in early 1941.

At the time of Ingersoll's visit, the British were quite confident of their ability to hold their position at Singapore if not Hong Kong. They planned to base a battle fleet at Singapore if the Japanese moved south. If Germany and Italy became hostile at the same time, however, British forces in the Far East would have to be reduced. On the occasion of Ingersoll's visit it was the Americans who were taking the initiative in seeking assurances of Allied cooperation. But by May 1939, the British were so concerned over the German and Italian threat in the Mediterranean as well as in the rest of the Atlantic area that the Admiralty sent a staff officer to Washington to inform the Navy's War Plans Division that they now considered it impossible to send a strong battle force to Singapore. They were hopeful that the U.S. Navy would accept the task of defending the Malay Barrier.[1] Admiral Leahy could make no commitments, but he did venture a personal opinion. In a global war he envisioned the U.S. Fleet's controlling the Pacific while the Allied Fleet controlled the European waters, the Mediterranean, and the Atlantic.

---

[1] Morison, The Rising Sun, pp. 49 - 50; Morton, Chap. iii, p. 2.

Aid to Britain versus Build-up at Home

Four months later Europe was at war. During the first nine months of the war little was done toward increasing the strength of the U.S. armed forces or toward assisting or collaborating with the Western Allies. Under the terms of the Neutrality Act of November 1939, anyone could buy munitions in the United States who had the money. The Navy kept its main force in the Pacific but established a "neutrality patrol" in the Western Atlantic. The Army grew slowly from about 190,000 to about 245,000; and on 22 May 1940, Admiral Stark was highly gratified to write Admiral Richardson: "Thank God, yesterday I finally swung support for 170,000 men and 34,000 marines."[1]

After Poland and Czechoslovakia were absorbed by Germany and Russia, after Finland was defeated and Denmark and Norway occupied, and while the Baltic States were being prepared for destruction, the war in the west became a "phoney war." But it became real indeed in May and June of 1940. At once the United States began, in the words of President Roosevelt,

> to extend to the opponents of force the material resources of this nation and at the same time, . . . harness and speed up the use of those resources in order that we ourselves in the Americas may have equipment and training equal to the task of any emergency and every defense.[2]

The two objectives of extending aid and building up the Army and Navy, however, were in sharp conflict with one another. The national

---

[1] Personal letter reproduced in *Pearl Harbor Hearings*, Exhibit No. 7.

[2] Quoted by Richard M. Leighton and Robert W. Coakley, *Global Logistics and Strategy, 1940-1943* (Washington: U.S. Government Printing Office, 1955), p. 28.

leadership, civil and military, was sorely tried in the coming months in an attempt to reconcile the demands of the two. After Britain stood alone, no one doubted her urgent need for outside assistance but forecasts of her survival were often pessimistic, and there was great resistance at times to investing in a lost cause. The President, personally and constantly, had to intervene to keep assistance flowing to those embattled isles.[1] The most dramatic example of aid during the period was the exchange in early September 1940 of fifty old destroyers to Britain for long term leases to a number of base sites on British territory in the Western Atlantic.[2] This was managed by the President under his authority to dispose of surplus munitions. Not until December, however, did he announce his plan for lend-lease legislation. And in his fireside chat of 29 December he popularized this whole program with his description of America's role as the arsenal of democracy.[3]

In the meantime strategic planning had continued apace with events. As already seen, the planners were finding increasing need for coordination of U.S. plans with the British, and this coordination needed to be preceded by the establishment of a firm national policy.

---

[1] Watson, Chaps. x and xi for an account of this struggle.

[2] For a full account of this transaction see Conn and Fairchild, Chap. ii. See also Watson, pp. 306, 368 - 69, 478.

[3] Leighton and Coakley, pp. 44 - 45. Lend-lease became law on 11 March 41.

The need for coordination was felt even more urgently in Britain, at all levels of the government. Immediately after being called to lead the government, Mr. Churchill, writing as a "former naval person," continued his personal correspondence with Mr. Roosevelt which had begun while he was First Lord of the Admiralty.[1] In his letter of 15 May 1940 he set forth the non-belligerent help Britain needed from America in her stand against Germany. He also made it clear that he counted on the United States "to keep the Japanese quiet in the Pacific, using Singapore in any way convenient." In June the Admiralty named a committee headed by Sir Sidney Bailey to conduct a comprehensive review of the kind of assistance needed and the areas where coordination of U.S.-British plans was necessary, and to recommend means of effecting the coordination. Thereafter, through diplomatic and military channels in both London and Washington, there came a series of suggestions for initiating military staff conversations. The British Ambassador, Lord Lothian, recalled the success of Admiral William S. Sims, USN, as a Special Naval Observer in London during World War I and recommended to the President that a senior naval officer again be sent to London with a similar mission.

Military Liaison Extended

The idea was well received by the President and by the two service departments. In fact it was decided to send two army officers also, but for a shorter period of duty. The officers selected were Rear

---

[1] This began with Roosevelt's letter of 11 Sep 39. See Winston S. Churchill, *The Second World War*, 6 vols. (Boston: Houghton Mifflin Company, 1948-55), I, 440 - 41 and II, 22 - 25.

Admiral Robert L. Ghormley, an Assistant Chief of Naval Operations; Brigadier General George V. Strong, Chief of War Plans Division; and Major General Delos C. Emmons, Commanding General of the GHQ Air Force.[1]

Thus, at last, the informal liaison between the naval establishments of the two countries was broadened to include the other services. The interchange of ideas at the ensuing conversations in August and September was extremely valuable. Admiral of the Fleet Sir Dudley Pound, First Sea Lord; General Sir John Dill, Chief of the Imperial General Staff; and Air Chief Marshal Sir Cyril L. Newell, Chief of the Air Staff, all spoke with frankness. Especially interesting to the Americans were the conceptions of the British military leaders of the proper strategy to be employed in the war. First of all they made it clear that Germany was the main enemy. Action anywhere must therefore be related to the supreme military objective of defeating Germany. Ultimately, highly mobile, largely armored army forces would have to be employed; sea and air power were not sufficient by themselves. Although they held high hopes of defeating the great air offensive just being launched by the Luftwaffe, they nevertheless hoped that their own eventual air offensive would be so effective as to render less formidable the Army's delivery of the coup de grace.

---

[1] Minutes of Meetings, Anglo-American Standardization of Arms Committee, and related papers in WPD 4402-1. This is a part of one large folder of papers with file numbers, 4402 and 4402-1 to 4402-20. Material also covers the staff conferences in Washington in Jan-Mar 41 and in Singapore in April, 1941 discussed below.

With the loss of the French Fleet and the entry into the war of Italy, it was no longer possible for the British to send a fleet to Singapore to meet an attack by the Japanese. If a portion of the U.S. Fleet were sent to the Atlantic, the force at Gibralter could release perhaps two capital ships to the Indian Ocean but not to Singapore. To be effective at Singapore, a much stronger force would have to be sent, and that could not be done.

As the coversations drew to a close, General Strong observed that it had been generally agreed that a periodical exchange of information was desirable and that he himself thought that the exchange should be placed upon a regular basis.[1]

Some American Views

An Army Estimate

On 25 September, less than a month after returning to Washington, and just two days before Japan finally joined the European Axis Powers in the Tripartite Pact, General Strong submitted a comprehensive strategic estimate in a memorandum with the long but descriptive subject title: The Problem of Production of Munitions in Relation to the Ability of the United States to Cope with its Defense Problems in the Present World Situation.[2] The ten page memorandum was the

---

[1] Mins of Mtg, 31 Aug 40.
[2] Copy in WPD 4321-91.

result of a study by a group of both naval and army officers. Although they recognized the possibility of a simultaneous attack by all three of the Axis Powers, they concluded that Germany and Italy could not attack immediately. Nevertheless, they reviewed, in turn, the immediate danger of accelerated infiltration into South America; the less probable but more dangerous contingency of an Axis capture of Gibralter and perhaps Dakar; and, finally, the loss of the British Fleet. Possible defensive actions which the United States might take to meet these various situations, such as protective seizure of bases in the Atlantic and Caribbean, were already provided for in RAINBOW 1 and 4.

They turned then to the Pacific, where an attack seemed much more likely. Very soon the nation might be faced with the alternatives of reversing its policy of unyielding opposition to Japan's expansion or of meeting force with force. To meet any of these situations, in the Atlantic or the Pacific, the United States had too few men, and these were insufficiently supplied with munitions.

Implied in this thoughtful paper was a strong plea for time, a plea from the military leaders which would be heard often and with a growing insistence during the next fourteen and one half months of peace.[1] Yet just ten days later at a meeting of the Standing Liaison Committee,[2] Mr. Welles presented for consideration a

---

[1] See, e.g. Hull, <u>Memoirs</u>, pp. 107, 176, 86.

[2] This committee was organized in early 1938, apparently at the instance of Secretary Hull. It was composed of the CofS, CNO, and Hull's undersecretary, Sumner Welles. In his words it "would be charged with the study of coordination and liaison both at home

message from Mr. Churchill requesting that a naval squadron be sent to Singapore. The Committee quickly decided that such a move was more a provocation than a deterrent. Admiral Stark was moved to say that "every day we are able to maintain peace and still support the British is valuable time gained." General Marshall asserted that it was "as unfavorable a moment as you could choose" for such action.[1] Going further, he recommended the immediate withdrawal of the Marines from Shanghai since it was "inconceivable" that they should avoid attack. General Strong, who was present, said he doubted if the President had read his strategic estimate of 25 September "which had been drafted as a basis for formulating policy." Mr. Welles agreed to attempt to get presidential action in the matter.

During the same month of October the British again proposed, and again through both diplomatic and military channels, new and more comprehensive staff conversations. Coming on the eve of the third term elections, the President declined to approve the proposals at that time.[2] But on 13 November he received such a proposal again, this time from Admiral Stark in what came to be known as his plan Dog Memorandum.[3]

---

and abroad of the three departments concerned, and of the Foreign Service and the two combatant services. Matters of national policy affecting the three departments would also be taken up and discussed by the Committee." Despite these brave words, the value of its work was limited. See Watson, pp. 89 - 91. Strangely, in Mr. Hull's two-volume memoirs he fails to mention the committee a single time.

[1] Watson, p. 117.

[2] See Watson's speculations on this point, *Ibid.*, p. 19 and n. 20.

[3] Familiarly so called because of the crucial par. "D" ("Dog" in the military phonetic alphabet), discussed below.

The Plan Dog Memorandum

On 4 November, Admiral Stark had attempted to crystallize his personal views by putting them down on paper in the form of a memorandum to the Secretary of the Navy. In the process he worked the clock around, coming to grips with strategic problems around the globe, relating them to one another and to American policy, and reaching some boldly expressed conclusions. He sent a copy of his memorandum to General Marshall, inviting his comments, and then called in a number of his closest advisers to help him revise it.[1] Eight more days of labor did little more than clarify some of the wording, adding three more pages to the original twenty-three.[2] The result was a rambling, discursive paper, which was, without doubt, the most comprehensive and authoritative expression of the Navy's views on strategy recorded in the immediate prewar period. Although it was only one link in a long chain of events, it was an especially significant link. It helped fix the direction of future joint planning and initiated a new planning phase which culminated two and one half months later in the most important British and American staff

---

[1] On the day it was completed, Adm Stark wrote to Adm Richardson at Pearl Harbor saying he had been helped by "Ingersoll, Turner, Savvy /Cooke/, Charlie Welborn, Forrest Sherman, Hill, Sexton, Moore, and Oscar Badger." Most of these officers would have great responsibilities for the next five years in the development and execution of strategy, especially in the Pacific. Copy of ltr in Pearl Harbor Hearings, Exhibit 9.

[2] A copy of the revised memorandum, dated 12 Nov 40, with related papers prepared in the War Dept, is in WPD 4175-15.

conference prior to the war.

The sweep of Admiral Stark's memorandum and much of its reasoning is reminiscent of the RAINBOW studies two years earlier. It also bears some resemblance to General Strong's estimate of 25 September. Both Strong and Stark thought that the greatest potential danger was in the Atlantic but that the most imminent danger was in the Pacific. Both, too, recognized the role of the British Fleet in the defense of the Western Hemisphere. But where Strong, conservative and perhaps more pessimistic (there was greater reason for pessimism than there was six weeks later) was more concerned with the danger and resulting problems of a British collapse, Stark was concerned with means of preventing that collapse. Admiral Stark did think that the British were too optimistic about ultimate success. He was convinced that victory over Germany could be assured only by a successful offensive on land. But Britain was clearly unable to launch such an offensive alone. In such an undertaking the United States would have to participate with strong land as well as air and naval forces.

In order to carry out the necessary commitments in the Atlantic, Stark argued, U.S. forces could not engage in an unlimited war in the Pacific. An ORANGE-type war "could require several years and the absorption of the full military, naval, and economic energy of the American people." After finally destroying the external military power of Japan and starving her economically, it would still be necessary, in order to keep her in check, to retain and develop an adequate base in the Far East; and this would be a reversal of a long-standing American policy.

Even a limited war, Stark warned, often had a way of becoming unlimited. A strong commitment toward a westward advance in the Mandates would invite an increasing concentration of effort in that drive. Moreover, it would be extremely difficult, prestige-damaging, and perhaps even disastrous to withdraw if it later became necessary to shift emphasis to the Atlantic.

What was needed was a firm and clear decision on national policy, one which could then be pursued by the mutually supporting diplomatic and military services of the nation. What needed to be answered, said Admiral Stark, was the question: "Where shall we fight and for what objective"? The answer lay in the choice among four possible strategies:

(a) Concentration on Hemisphere Defense.

(b) All-out offense, in company with British and Dutch forces, against Japan; strict defense in the Atlantic.

(c) Strongest possible assistance to allies in both Europe and the Far East.

(d) Main effort in the Atlantic; defense in the Pacific.

Admiral Stark then proceeded to discuss the advantages and disadvantages of each of the four strategies (plans, he called them). The overriding weakness of the first three was that if any of them were adopted, Britain could not defeat Germany and perhaps could not even survive. Even the adoption of Plan D would not guarantee success, but it offered the best chances, "particularly," said Stark, "if we insist upon full equality in the political and military direction of the war." And that statement led to a strong recommendation for staff conferences with the British in London, the Canadians in Washington, and the British and Dutch in Singapore.

General Marshall and his officers in WPD were in substantial agreement with the conclusion and recommendations of the memorandum.[1] Colonel J. W. Anderson, Acting Chief of WPD, gave the Chief of Staff a critique of the original 4 November memorandum, copies of which Marshall sent to Secretary Stimson and Admiral Stark on 13 November. On the same date Admiral Stark sent a copy of his revised memorandum, along with a copy of the Army's critique to the President.[2] The only objections of substance which the Army had were reflections of its more conservative outlook. In the Atlantic it was less inclined to make an all-out commitment to the British Empire, and in the Pacific it was opposed even to considering any offensive action west of Hawaii. Said Colonel Anderson in the critique:

---

[1] Memo, CofS for Sec War, 13 Nov 40, WPD 4175-15.

[2] Ibid.; a copy of the critique is also in WPD 4175-16.

If accepted as presented, it is believed that the United States would be committed to a course of action which would eventually involve an unlimited war in the Atlantic plus at the minimum a limited objective war in the Pacific. War Plans Division believes it is extremely dangerous to even intimate that all of the stated national objectives can be sustained simultaneously.

Nevertheless, one month later the Army and Navy planners had revised Admiral Stark's memorandum to their mutual satisfaction and submitted it to the Joint Board as a joint estimate. The President had recently requested a joint War, State and Navy estimate. General Marshall preferred sending this estimate directly from the Joint Board to the White House, perhaps with the concurrence of the Liaison Committee. But in the end he accepted Admiral Stark's suggestion to try to have it approved by the three secretaries and sent forward by them.[1]

On 3 January 1941 the two service chiefs and their two chief planning officers, General Gerow and Captain Turner conferred with Mr. Hull in his office. Hull presumably had already discussed the estimate with Sumner Welles, a member of the Standing Liaison Committee.[2] He thought the paper was an excellent analysis of the situation and in general accord with his own views. He nevertheless felt it inappropriate for the Secretary of State to join in sponsoring a technical military statement. He was interested in the views of the two military leaders, however, and discussed with them at some

---

[1] Memo, Stark for Marshall, 22 Nov 40; Memo, Gerow for CofS, 16 Dec 40; Memo, Gerow for CofS, 20 Dec 40; Comment on Disposition Slip by Lt Col O. Ward, SGS, no date. All in WPD 4175-15.

[2] Resume of the conference in Memo from Gen Gerow to the CofS, sub: Conference with the Secretary of State, 3 Jan 41, in WPD 4175-15.

length the problems of avoiding war, policies which might lead to war, and the merits of participating in the war versus aid to Britain short of war.

During the conference General Marshall and Admiral Stark attempted to convince Mr. Hull that their paper was more than a technical military statement, that it recommended a policy involving "broad national questions as well as those pertaining to military and naval operations."[1] Before the Army and Navy and then the American and British military leaders could cooperate effectively in detailed planning, a definite stand in these matters had to be taken by the government. Mr. Hull was not persuaded by these arguments and so he forfeited perhaps his last good chance for effective participation in shaping wartime strategy. He was later to complain many times for being excluded from the great wartime conferences between the heads of governments and their military advisers.[2]

Shortly afterwards, Mr. Stimson discussed with Mr. Hull the estimate and the matter of coordinating State, War, and Navy Department policies. They agreed that thereafter the three secretaries would meet each Tuesday to discuss national defense matters.[3] This

---

[1] As summarized by Gen Gerow, Ibid.

[2] Hull, p. 1109.

[3] Handwritten note by Gen Marshall at end of Gen Gerow's memo of 3 Jan 41, cited above.

arrangement effectively superseded the two year old Standing Liaison Committee, although the latter remained active for a period longer.

The President Decides

The policy guidance which the military chiefs had been seeking came directly from the President on 16 January 1941. On that day he called to the White House the two service chiefs and the Secretaries of War, Navy, and State, a group known informally as the "War Council." He opined that there was an outside chance of a simultaneous attack by the three Axis Powers and that it could come at any time. Consequently, he admonished his advisers, war plans should be kept up to date, reflecting always what could be done immediately. He implied that the RAINBOW Plans were not entirely realistic, in that respect.[1]

He emphasized his strong desire to be able to assure Mr. Churchill that aid to Britain would continue unabated even if the Axis attacked the United States. He would thus thwart the very design of Hitler in involving the United States in the war. He asked that the planners bear this in mind and to plan on the basis that England could last at least six months and that at least two additional months would pass before the Axis could attack the Western Hemisphere. Moreover, he wanted the Navy prepared to escort convoys to England and to patrol

---

[1] The conference was summarized the next day by Gen Marshall in a memo to Gen Gerow, filed in WPD 4175-18.

off-shore from Maine to the Virginia Capes.[1] The policy for employing the Army, however, should be conservative until its strength was developed. He did not expect it to be prepared to send moderately strong forces to assist any friendly Latin American government threatened by Nazi inspired movements.

In the Pacific the United States would stand on the defensive with the U.S. Fleet based in Hawaii. The Asiatic Fleet would remained based in the Philippines. It would not be reinforced and when forced to retire, would move east or to Singapore at the discretion of its commander.

These verbal instructions by the President were just the kind needed, whether or not they satisfied all the personal preferences of the military leaders. The President displayed an understanding of the points of view of both services, synthesizing and compromising them into remarkable fashion. He must have indeed seen and read carefully General Strong's estimate of 25 September as well as Admiral Stark's more recent memorandum and the joint estimate developed from it.

Pre-War Conferences

ABC-1[2]

Army and Navy leaders were now better prepared for the approaching

---

[1] There was some question about this, as Marshall noted in his memo. The patrol actually operated far south of the Virginia Capes.

[2] The American-British staff conversations held in Washington between 2 Feb and 24 Mar 41 and the final report of the conversations were thereafter commonly referred to by the short title ABC-1.

staff conferences with representatives of the British Chiefs of Staff. The President's views on strategy were compatible if not identical to theirs, and his directive left them with great freedom for working out the details of an allied strategy.

Word came from London on 2 December that British staff officers would soon arrive in Washington.[1] The President apparently had approved the conversations through diplomatic channels without close coordination with the service departments. There was no disharmony, however, between the commander in chief and his military advisers. The Joint Planning Committee had already drawn up recommended instructions for the American representatives three days before the 16 January conference. After going through the hands of the Joint Board and the service secretaries, the President approved them with only minor changes on 26 January.[2] The instructions included a recommended agenda and a "Statement by the Chief of Naval Operations and the Chief of Staff." The "Statement" reiterated the firm and long-held conviction that in a global war the main objectives of the associated (changed by the President from "Allied") powers must be the defeat of Germany. If at all possible, war with Japan should be avoided. If not possible, operations against Japan should be so

---

[1] Memo, Col McNarney to Gen Gerow, sub: Staff Conversations, 2 Dec 41, WPD 4402.

[2] Private and Confidential Memo, F.D.R. to Sec Navy, 26 Jan 41, copy in WPD 4402-2.

conducted as not to divert the main effort away from the European area.[1]

The Grand Alliance of the United States and the United Kingdom was probably the most successful of its kind in history. It had a solid foundation of mutual interests and a common heritage to build on and leaders who learned to respect and to trust one another. Yet there was bound to remain throughout the war some inhibitions in their relations, some residual amounts of mistrust. No document in the military files of the war reveals more clearly and succinctly the reservations toward this Grand Alliance in the mind of the American High Command than did the covering memorandum by which the Planners forwarded their recommended agenda and "Statement" to the Joint Board. In it the U.S. representatives were reminded that

> recent British political and military leadership has not been outstanding with the exception of Prime Minister Churchill's leadership, Admiral Cunningham's command of the Mediterranean Fleet, and General Wavell's command of the British Force in Egypt.

Moreover, the United States, if necessary, could

> safeguard the North American Continent and probably the Western Hemisphere, whether allied with Britain or not.

Therefore the nation need not and ought not "intrust [its] . . . future to British direction."[2]

---

[1] Memo, J.B. 325, JPC to JB, sub: Joint Instructions for Army and Navy Representatives . . . , 13 Jan 41, incl the recommended agenda and the "Statement," WPD 4402-1; Memo for Record, Lt Col Scobey, same sub, 27 Jan 41; Memo, CofS, for Adm Stark, same sub, 27 Jan 41. The last two in WPD 4402-2. A copy of the "Statement" is in Pearl Harbor Hearings, Exhibit 43. See also Morton, Chap. iii, p. 33.

[2] Supra,. p.   , Adm Stark's insistence upon "full equality in the political and military direction of the war." Also infra, p.   , regarding the agreed policy on command.

Army and Navy officers were clearly skeptical of British hopes of so weakening Germany with their air and naval forces that the Army's task would be one simply of delivering the <u>coup de grace</u>. They generally agreed that Britain could not

> encompass the defeat of Germany unless the United States provides that nation with military assistance, plus a far greater degree of material aid than is given now; and that, even then, success against the Axis is not assured.

They then cautioned that

> it is to be expected that proposals of the British representatives will have been drawn up with chief regard for the support of the British Commonwealth. Never absent from British minds are their post-war interests, commercial and military. We should likewise safeguard our own eventual interests.

Finally,

> in order to avoid commitment by the President neither he nor any of his cabinet should officially receive the British officers . . . /but they should/ be informally received by the Undersecretary of State, the Chief of Naval Operations, and the Chief of Staff, substantially as proposed in the program.

A British staff committee arrived on 25 January and the first formal meeting with them was held five days later. Altogether fourteen meetings were held over a period of two months.[1]

For the Atlantic and European areas, where the interests of the two nations were largely the same, the conference agreed on general

---

[1] The American representatives were, for the Army, Maj Gen S. D. Embick, Brig Gen Sherman Miles, Brig Gen L. T. Gerow, and Col J. T. McNarney; for the Navy, Rear Adm R. L. Ghormley, Rear Adm R. K. Turner, Capt A. G. Kirk, Capt C. M. Cooke, Jr., and Capt D. C. Ramsey. A copy of the final rpt, dated 27 Mar 41 is in <u>Pearl Harbor Hearings</u>, Exhibit 49, Part 15, pp. 1485 - 1542; related papers are in OPD Exec O. Files, Item 11, Exec 4 and in WPD 4402-1.

principles fairly easily and early. Defense of other large areas of the globe, such as the Indian and Pacific Oceans, were clearly the primary responsibility of one or another of the two. They both had important interests in the Far East but they were not the same nor of equal importance. Consequently there were sharp differences over the defense of that area. The key to its defense, thought the British, was Singapore. The Americans criticized this largely in terms of grand tactics, but their real objections were to an all-out defense of any kind in the Far East. American planners had long before conceded the impossibility of defending the Philippines. This "impossibility" was a practical and not an absolute one however. With Midway, Wake, and Guam adequately fortified to protect the line of communication, with Cavite developed into a major naval base, and with a strong garrison of air and ground forces, the Islands could certainly have been defended. But these defenses did not exist, and time had run out in trying to create them. More vital areas were also poorly defended, and their needs had to be met first.

It was different for the British. They depended heavily upon the resources of Malaysia, and if strategic Singapore fell, all of Malaysia would go, Australia and India would be exposed, and even the Near East would be more vulnerable.

The final agreement on the Far East policy did not compromise the American stand. It declared that if Japan does enter the war, the military strategy in the Far East will be defensive. The United States does not intend to add to its present military strength in the Far East but will employ the United States Pacific Fleet offensively in the manner best calculated to weaken Japanese economic power and to support the defense of the Malay barrier by diverting Japanese strength away from Malaysia. The United States intends to so augment its forces in the Atlantic and Mediterranean areas that the British Commonwealth will be in a position to release the necessary forces to the Far East.

What ultimately had to be compromised was the difference in the U.S. Army and the U.S. Navy's interpretation of offensive fleet operations. Annex III of ABC-1 charged the Fleet with the capture of positions in the Marshalls and the conduct of raids westward from Hawaii in order to divert Japanese strength away from Malaysia. Army land and air forces operations were to be purely defensive. Yet not long after the war started army planners would complain that every move by the Navy seemed to include the need for seizing land areas and the use of resources of the Army.[1]

An important provision of the agreement was for the exchange of military missions in the event of war and for the immediate exchange of the nucleuses of those missions. Significantly, the missions were to be corporate bodies, representing their military chiefs jointly. This precedent was already being established at ABC-1, at which American officers were representing General Marshall and Admiral Stark jointly. This had not been the case at previous conferences.

1
  Infra, p.

It was preferable, thought the conferees, for the forces of one nation to operate in their own area of responsibility. The United States would be responsible for virtually all the Pacific and the western half of the Atlantic. Unity of command (presumably under a Supreme War Council) would be established for offensive land campaigns. Other theaters would be the responsibility of the British.

Remembering, no doubt, the difficulties of General Pershing in France, the conferees agreed that forces of one power employed under the strategic direction of another would operate as a task force, or task forces, under their own command. This arrangement would be temporarily suspended only in exceptional circumstances.

In the Far East, depending upon agreement by the Dutch, each power would defend its own territory. Naval forces of the associated powers would be under the command of the British Naval Commander-in-Chief, China, except those forces defending the Philippines.

The United States-British Commonwealth Joint Basic War Plan Number One was attached to the report as Annex III. Taking up one area after another around the globe, it allocated forces and assigned tasks. It was recognized at the start that its provisions were subject to the strategic situation at the time that the United States, Japan, and the Netherlands East Indies might enter into the war. And, like the whole report, it did not constitute a political agreement.

Remembering the injunction of the President of 16 January, the assigned forces were those currently available. It was noted, however, that accession to the U.S. Fleet during the next two months would include one battleship, one aircraft carrier, ten submarines, and one submarine minelayer.

A. D. B.

The next month (21 - 27 April) representatives of the American, Dutch and British commanders met at Singapore to work out more detailed plans for cooperating in the Far East under the provisions of ABC-1. The short title of this conference and of its final report is A.D.B. The planning environment in Singapore was different from Washington. The views of the Joint Board were seriously compromised at Singapore. Despite the clear statements in ABC-1, officers in the Far East, Americans included, hoped for greater reinforcement of their forces, and the British and Dutch were more persuasive in advocating a strong defense of the Malay Barrier, anchored on Singapore. The British and Dutch efforts to commit the United States shows through in such statements of the final report as the following:

> The Associated Powers are convinced that any attack against one is of vital importance for the others.

and

> Knowledge by Japan that aggression by her against one of the Associated Powers would immediately lead to united resistance by all might prevent war.

In addition, there was a recommendation that a combined naval staff be established at Singapore immediately.

There were repeated acknowledgements that, in the event of a global war, the main effort would be in the Atlantic. Yet the conferees saw a number of actions, offensive in themselves, which could be carried out in defense of the interests of the democracies. They included in this operations in the Marshalls and Carolines by the Pacific Fleet, but they were less than certain that this would draw Japanese strength away from Malaysia.

They also recommended organizing and supporting guerrilla forces in China. Britain had already begun organizing subversive activities, sabotage, and corruption in Japan and occupied territories; and the other Powers were invited to join in this effort.

Japan would ultimately be defeated, they thought, by "economic blockade, naval pressure, and air bombardment." These measures should therefore be started early. Luzon could furnish air and submarine bases for these offensive operations and its defenses, therefore, should be strengthened.

Yet, somewhat contradictory to this recommendation, was one that submarines, destroyers, large patrol plane tenders, and tankers be sent from Manila to Singapore before hostilities if the situation should become "threatening."

Powerful counterattacks would begin after the arrival of the British Far Eastern Fleet at Singapore.[1]

---

[1] A summary of the conference and related papers are in WPD 4402-18; the final report is printed in Pearl Harbor Hearings, Exhibit 50.

General Marshall and Admiral Stark objected to the report of the conference in many major and minor particulars.[1] One serious matter was the inclusion of political matters outside the province of the service departments. Another was the great reliance on U.S. naval forces in the defense of the Malay Barrier compared to the negligible British naval forces. The arrival of a British Far Eastern Fleet was "problematical," and the creation in the meantime of an Eastern Theater and a Commander-in-Chief, Far Eastern Fleet, was of questionable value. Besides criticisms of other command relations, Admiral Stark was emphatic in refusing the use of U.S. naval aviation for other than naval purposes.

Especially interesting were the military chiefs' remarks about the Philippines. While they objected to the role A.D.B. assigned the Philippines, their objections were softened by words and phrases which presaged an early change in U.S. policy:

> Because of the greater needs of other strategic areas, the United States is <u>not now</u> able to provide any considerable additional reinforcement to the Philippines. Under <u>present</u> World conditions, it is not considered possible to hope to launch a strong offensive from the Philippines. The United States is taking steps to strengthen the defense of the Philippines through improving the quality of native troops and by providing additional modern material.[2]

---

[1] Set forth in a six page message to the Special Army and Naval Observers in London, 3 Jul 41, copy in WPD 4402-18 and in <u>Pearl Harbor Hearings</u>, Exhibit 65.

[2] Emphasis added. See also ltr, Stark to Cooke, 31 Jul 41, in <u>Pearl Harbor Hearings</u>, Exhibit 100.

Finally, said Marshall and Stark, A.D.B. was not a plan at all. It was more a statement of hopes and concepts and full of inappropriate recommendations.

Some of the differences were cleared up the next month at the Atlantic Conference, others were settled later, and still others were unresolved when war came to the Pacific.[1]

The Atlantic Conference

The next month the service chiefs of the United States and the United Kingdom met face to face for the first time. The occasion was the meeting 9 - 15 August of Roosevelt and Churchill just off Argentina, Newfoundland. The main purpose of the meeting was to define and then to announce the aims of the two democracies in opposing the Axis Powers. Military discussions did not produce any important decisions -- nor was this expected. The exchange did bring into sharper focus some of the differences in points of view and allowed the military leaders to take the measure of their counterparts.[2]

RAINBOW 5

Work on RAINBOW 5 had not awaited the outcome of the A.D.B. and Argentina Conference. Work on it had begun in May 1940, but the defeat of France and the precarious position of Britain forced the

---
[1] See exchange of correspondence between London and Washington during Sep, Oct, and Nov 41 in WPD 4402-18.
[2] See Watson, pp. 400 - 06.

attention of American planners back to problems of Hemisphere Defense (RAINBOW 4) and possible war against Japan (RAINBOW 3). As the situation improved, a modified RAINBOW 5 situation once again seemed to be the one for which the United States should prepare. But by then informal American-British staff conversations were under way and others were being planned.

Stark and Marshall gave tentative approval to ABC-1 a few days after the conference ended and immediately directed that a new Joint RAINBOW 5 be prepared, based on the agreements of the conference. The new joint plan was completed quickly, for it was little more than a copy of ABC-1. The Joint Board approved both on 14 May, Secretary of Navy Knox approved it on 28 May and Secretary Stimson on 2 June. The President studied the plans and asked that they be returned to him for approval in case of war.[1] With that the two services commenced developing their own basic war plans RAINBOW 5.

The joint plan was not an operational plan for the defeat of the Axis Powers. This was impossible, simply because of the situation at the beginning of hostilities could not be predicted. Only an aggressor could do that, and then only with caution. Nor was the plan unambiguous. For example, the following were listed at one point "as the principal offensive policies against the Axis Powers" included in "the strategic concept" of the plan:

    (a) Application of economic pressure by naval, land, and sea forces and all other means, including the control of the commodities at their source by diplomatic and financial measures.

    (b) A sustained air offensive against German military power, supplemented by air offensives against other regions under enemy control which contribute to that power.

---

[1] Morton, Chap. iii, p. 41.

(c) The early elimination of Italy as an active partner in the Axis.

(d) The employment of the air, land and naval forces of the Associated Powers, at every opportunity, in raids and minor offensives against Axis military strength.

(e) The support of neutrals and of Allies of the United Kingdom, Associates of the United States, and populations in Axis-occupied territory in resistance to the Axis Powers,

(f) The building up of the necessary forces for an eventual offensive against Germany.

(g) The capture of positions from which to launch the eventual offensive. [1]

Some of these seemed more like objectives than policies; some, e.g. (a), (d), and (g) were susceptible of greatly different interpretations; and there was no paragraph (h) concerning the "eventual offensive" itself. Then there was the statement that

> The building up of large land and air forces for major offensive operations against the Axis Powers will be the primary immediate effort of the United States Army. The initial task of land and air forces will be limited to such operations as will not materially delay this effort.

If this was intended to apply only to the Atlantic and European theaters, it did not explicitly so state.

General tasks to be undertaken to "defeat the Axis Powers and guard the United States interests" were repetitious and listed in a curious order. They were the following:

a. Reducing Axis economic power to wage war, by blockade, raids, and a sustained air offensive;

b. Destroying Axis military power by raids and an eventual land, naval, and air offensive;

---

[1] From Sec IV of the Joint RAINBOW 5. A copy of Navy Basic War Plan - RAINBOW No. 5 is in Pearl Harbor Hearings; Exhibit 129. The Joint plan is included as Appendix I of the Navy Plan.

c. Protecting the sea communication of the Associated Powers;

d. Preventing the extension in the Western Hemisphere of European or Asiatic military power, and . . .

e. Protecting outlying military base areas and islands of strategic importance against land, sea, or sea-borne attack.

Least clear were the objectives in the Pacific and tasks assigned army and naval forces in operations against Japan. Constantly reaffirmed was the decision on that "if Japan does enter the war, the Military strategy in the Far East will be defensive." But elsewhere the authors of the plan had very carefully distinguished the "Far East" from the much larger Pacific and Australian-New Zealand areas. This may have implied approval of offensive operations in the larger area. Even in the Far East the Navy was directed to operate "offensively in the manner best calculated to weaken Japanese economic power and to support the defense of the Malay barrier by diverting Japanese strength away from Malaysia." The Navy was also directed to protect the sea communications of the Associated Powers in the Pacific and Far East Areas and to cooperate with the British in the Southwest Pacific almost to the coast of Australia. These responsibilities were later interpreted as authorizing some rather ambitious offensive operations. The Navy expected to make some initial landings in the Marshalls six months after the start of hostilities in preparation for further moves westward.

The Army was directed to support the Navy in the task of protecting the lines of communication. Its leaders, however, did not expect the Army to "furnish garrisons for any islands or bases in the Pacific under Rainbow V, other than those now occupied." Marines were to be used in the "seizure and defense of temporary bases in the Pacific Area." For fear of implying otherwise, they carefully avoided joining the Navy in discussing with the British the problems of cooperating to protect the lines of communication to Australia.[1]

Strengthening the Pacific

Many developments conspired during the last few months of peace to change the American policy of not adding to its military strength in the Far East. The most important development was simply the increase in military means. Some historians have written about this change as if it represented a change of mind of the strategic planners about both the desirability and the feasibility of defending successfully the Philippines and other areas in the Western Pacific. The planners, themselves, especially Army planners were so zealous in maintaining the primacy of the Atlantic over the Pacific that at times they seemed to argue, as a matter of principle, against strengthening the defenses in the Western Pacific. But this reasoning was not evident in the many thoughtful studies and policy

---

[1] See pencilled notes to Lt Col Scobey, one from Lt Col Bundy, 22 May 41, the other from Gen Gerow, undated, both in WPD 4402-18.

statements prepared in prewar years. After July 1941 there was a feeling almost of embarrassment and apology in the change of policy, although this ought not have been so. The change in policy was not inconsistent with past views of the importance of American interests in the Far East or of the problems of defending those interests.[1]

Germany's attack on Russia on 22 June 1941 relieved the immediate threat somewhat to the Atlantic, making it easier to allot more resources to the defenses against Japan. At the same time it increased the needs in the Pacific, for Japan was immediately freed of some of the pressure exerted against her by Soviet forces in Siberia. The persistent requests from commanders in the Philippines and from Manuel Quezon, President of the Commonwealth, also had their influence.[2]

Another potent factor in the changing policy was the development of long-range bombardment aircraft and the belief that they could substitute for a stronger fleet. The presence of a strong fleet in the Philippines had always been a necessity, first, for the successful defense of the Islands, and, second, for conduct of offensive operations in the China and Philippine Seas. It was too late to develop a major naval base in the Philippines, even if there had been a will to do so. But the air power could be built up relatively quickly;

---

[1] See Watson, pp. 411 - 452, for a detailed development of this same idea. Also *supra*, p.

[2] Maj Gen George Grunert was CG, Phil Dept. Lt Gen Douglas MacArthur, former Chief of Staff and Military Adviser to the Commonwealth since 1936, was recalled to active duty in July 1941 and given command of all army forces in the Far East. Admiral Thomas C. Hart was C-in-C, Asistic Fleet.

it could perform both defensive and offensive tasks; and it could make up for the deficiencies of the Asiatic Fleet and complement the considerable capabilities which it did have.

The decision to strengthen the air forces in the Philippines stimulated interest in developing an air route less exposed than the one via Midway, Wake, and Guam. Approval to develop one via Christmas, Canton, Samoa, the Fijis, and New Caledonia was given in August and construction of bases at those points began in October 1941. This air route was expected also to provide additional security along the line of communication to the Southwest Pacific.[1]

Plans for the build-up of forces in the Philippines were projected through 1942. Although supply reserves would still be low and unit efficiency only moderately high (in the Commonwealth at least) defense forces would be near their maximum strength in March 1942. Now the great need was for more time, and the need was greater even than imagined. Admiral Stark, General Marshall, and their planners missed few opportunities in pleading for more.[2]

During the last months of peace the Asistic Fleet was augmented with a squadron of patrol bombers, 6 motor torpedo boats, and 18 submarines.[3] And on 5 November Admiral Stark was notified by the

---

[1] See Morton, Chap. iv, p. 13 and Wesley Frank Craven and James Lea Cate, eds., THE ARMY AIR FORCES IN WORLD WAR II, Vol. I, Plans and Early Operations, January 1939 to August 1942 (Chicago: The University of Chicago Press, 1948), pp. 180 - 82.

[2] See, e.g., Hull, pp. 1071, 1076, and 1087.

[3] Morton, Chap. iv, p. 16.

British Admiralty that a force of capital ships was finally being formed for the Far East and that Admiral Tom Phillips was en route to Singapore in H.M.S., *Prince of Wales* to take command.[1]

The general outlook was so optimistic during the fall that General MacArthur recommended that his mission be changed to the defense of the whole archipelago instead of Manila Bay alone. General Marshall approved the idea and recommended to the Joint Board that RAINBOW 5 be amended accordingly.[2]

But the few months additional time, so desperately needed, were not granted.

---

[1] Admiralty Most Secret Despatch 1559AS, 5 Nov 41, copy in WPD 4402-18.

[2] Correspondence on this matter and some related papers are in WPD 4175-15.

CHAPTER III

THE FIRST TWO YEARS OF WAR:
A STRATEGY OF ADJUSTMENT

On 7 December 1941 war came suddenly and violently to the Pacific. Japan exploited her initial success by proceeding at once to defeat in detail, the British, American, and Dutch forces in the Far East. The time, manner, and effectiveness of the Japanese attack and, thus, the resulting situation could not have been predicted in detail. Still, it was much as the planners had long assumed. Word was flashed from Washington for all commanders to prepare to execute RAINBOW 5. Just how it could have been executed in the Atlantic if Germany had not obligingly declared war four days later can be a matter of interesting speculation.

In the Far East General MacArthur and Admiral Hart needed three to ten more months' time to prepare for the defensive tasks assigned them by RAINBOW 5. And at Pearl Harbor the losses so weakened the offensive power of the Pacific Fleet that its attack on the Mandates was considerably delayed. This was a double misfortune for the defenders in the Far East, for the planned operations of the Pacific Fleet had been designed to assist them indirectly by drawing off Japanese strength and directly by guarding their lines of communication and by beginning the long movement of the center of military power from Hawaii westward.

But if some opportunities were lost, others were created by the new situation. Foremost among the new ones was the chance to exploit the new temper of the American people. The very boldness and success of Japan's initial operations united the public, not in despair but in enthusiastic defiance as nothing else could have. In addition, there was Australia, its northern coast only one third as far from Luzon as was Oahu. Australia had not figured at all in the old ORANGE planning and only lately had begun to figure in RAINBOW 5. Then there was MacArthur. His presence (later) in Australia was certain to introduce a new and significant ingredient in the developing strategy in the Pacific. To savor the full flavor of this assertion, one might imagine that MacArthur had been assigned to Hawaii instead of Australia after his evacuation from Luzon. What then would have been the route of advance toward Japan?

Desperate attempts were made to reinforce the defenders in the Philippines. But if years of ORANGE and RAINBOW planning served no other purpose, it enabled the military leaders to assess the situation realistically and to distinguish quickly and clearly between hopes and possibilities. The proper course of strategy was to adjust to the situation as it was, not as the planners or as the prewar plans would have it.

Resistance and reorganization were undertaken immediately and concurrently. After the momentum of the Japanese offensive was broken, counteroffensives would be undertaken, not, at first, in accordance with any long-range plan but simply directed against those Japanese positions which constituted the greatest immediate threat. Long-range planning (considered separately and in detail in the next chapter), it is true, was begun early in the war. It was an almost unbroken continuation of prewar planning, but the course of its development was influenced by the kind of Allied military organization adopted after Pearl Harbor, by the degree of success achieved in resisting Japan's early offensives, and by the lessons learned in the early Allied counter-offensives.

Organizing for Coalition War

Combined Chiefs of Staff

Shortly after Pearl Harbor Prime Minister Churchill brought his military chiefs and planners to Washington for the first of a series of wartime strategy conferences. This conference, known by its code name ARCADIA, was concerned with substantive questions of Allied strategy, but its greatest accomplishment was the establishment of an international military high command.[1] It considered but discarded the idea of creating an Allied War Council on the World War I model. Instead, the service chiefs of the two countries would compromise the Combined Chiefs of Staff, which would organize a permanent secretariat and a permanent planning staff. The Combined

---

[1] Churchill, *The Second World War*, III, pp. 686 - 87.

Chiefs of Staff (CCS) would be corporately responsible to the President and Prime Minister in much the same way as the British Joint Chiefs of Staff were already corporately responsible to Mr. Churchill in his dual capacity of Prime Minister and Minister of Defense.[1] The British suggested and the Americans agreed that the word "combined" would apply thereafter to international (American and British) activities and organizations and the word "joint" would apply to interservice activities and organizations of one nation. Cooperation with the others of the United Nations and development of a coordinated strategy with them would be effected by other and for the most part more conventional means of diplomatic and military liaison.[2]

Joint Chiefs of Staff

In the United States the means of developing joint Army-Navy strategy and for controlling its execution had not been institutionalized as it had been in Britain. The Joint Board of the Army and Navy had existed since 1903, but its effectiveness had varied through

---

[1] Cline, *Washington Command Post*, Chap. vi, esp. pp. 98 - 104, for an account of the development of the CCS; Morton, Chap. x, pp. 2 - 15 for a description of the JCS and of the planning organizations of the War and Navy Departments; *Federal Records of World War II*, Vol. II, already cited is also an excellent source, describing military organizations down to and including theaters and major field and fleet commands.

[2] United Nations was a term adopted at Roosevelt's suggestion. "Allied" might have created legal problems and "associated" was too flat.

the years, depending largely upon the cooperation of the Department of State and upon the interest of the President. Despite its many worthy accomplishments, it was inadequately organized and its functions were too limited for it to work effectively with the British Chiefs of Staff. It was largely in order to provide counterparts to the British membership in the CCS that the U.S. Joint Chiefs of Staff began to organize in early 1942 and to assume functions including and transcending those of the Joint Board. It was never formally chartered by law or directive, but its authority and effectiveness grew throughout the war. The Joint Board met rarely after this and was finally dissolved after World War II.

By the summer of 1942 the membership of the JCS was stabilized in the four men who were to retain their positions throughout the rest of the war. Admiral William D. Leahy, a former Chief of Naval Operations and, later, Governor of Puerto Rico and Ambassador to Vichy was recalled to active duty to fill the new position of Chief of Staff of the President in his capacity as Commander in Chief. In addition, he became chairman of the JCS. Other members were General George C. Marshall, Chief of Staff; Admiral Ernest J. King, who was by then both Commander in Chief, U.S. Fleet and Chief of Naval Operations;[1] and Lieutenant General Henry H. Arnold, the Commanding General, Army Air Forces. The Army Air Forces had gradually attained a semi-autonomous status within the Army, and

---

[1] Stark had been reassigned to command U.S. Naval Forces in Europe.

General Arnold's membership in the JCS and CCS further enhanced his prestige and independence and, hence, that of the organization which he headed. However, as Admiral Leahy had no command responsibilities and as General Arnold remained legally subordinate to General Marshall within the War Department, General Marshall and Admiral King were clearly the dominant members of the JCS throughout the war.

The Joint Chiefs relied on their Joint Staff Planners (JPS) for preparing both short-range and long-range plans as well as strategic studies. The Joint Planners numbered four and were senior officers on the planning staffs of the Army and Navy.[1] Individually, each directed the planning staff of his service, but for joint planning the planners relied primarily on the Joint War Plans Committee (JWPC).[2] This Committee in turn, was composed of a senior team and several permanent and ad hoc working teams. Usually there was at least one member of the Army, of the Navy, and of the Army Air Forces, and sometimes of the Marine Corps on each working team.

---

[1] From the late spring of 1942 onward the Army Planner was the Chief of the Strategy and Plans Group, Operations Division; the Army Air Planner was the Assistant Chief of Air Staff, Plans; and the two Navy Planners were the Assistant Chief of Staff, Plans, Office of the Commander in Chief, U.S. Fleet, and his Assistant Planning Officer (Air), Plans.

[2] Until the May 1943 reorganization, called the Joint U.S. Strategic Committee (JUSSC).

A number of planning groups with special cognizance in various technical and administrative fields were also assigned to the JCS. These groups included the Joint Logistics Committee, the Joint Communications Board, the Joint Military Transportation Committee, and the Joint Intelligence Committee, among others. Their function was to assist in keeping the strategic plans realistic and supportable and to develop the supporting administrative and logistic plans. Despite some apprehension over "the tail wagging the dog," they were not subordinated to the Joint Staff Planners but worked independently and on the same organizational level with them within the JCS.

Another committee of the JCS, one with a specially independent status was the Joint Strategic Survey Committee (JSSC). The members, who were often referred to as the military "elder statesmen," were Vice Admiral Russell Willson, USN, Ret, Lieutenant General Stanley D. Embick, USA, Ret, and Major General Muir S. Fairchild, USA, an air officer. The JSSC was assigned a variety of tasks which usually concerned problems of high strategy. Being men of wide experience and being freed from other responsibilities, the members of the JSSC brought unusual wisdom and objectivity to bear on their difficul problems. The Joint Chiefs continually sought their advice on important problems.

The Army Command Post

Within the War Department, strategic planning and strategic direction of army operations were centered in the Operations Division

(OPD).[1] The Strategy and Plans (S&P) Group of OPD was the group most concerned with joint and combined planning. S&P developed a number of basic strategic plans early in the war and frequently initiated studies on new strategic concepts. As the joint, the combined, and the theater planning staffs matured, however, the S&P group became more a review, coordinating and liaison organization. While the Army members of the JWPC were assigned administratively to the S&P Group, they performed their joint planning duties free from instructions from OPD.[2] However, OPD performed most of the staff work involved in drafting General Marshall's correspondence with Admiral King and thereby continued to have considerable influence on joint and combined planning. Also, OPD provided a training ground for the joint planners, for most army members of the JWPC served a tour in OPD.[3]

The Theater (Operations) Group of OPD, on the other hand, was mainly interested in current operational problems of the theaters.

---

[1] The old War Plans Division (WPD) became OPD soon after the reorganization of the Army in March 1942. See Cline, *Washington Command Post*, for a complete history of OPD in World War II and esp. Chap. iii for an account of its part in joint and combined planning. For the organization of the general staff prewar, see Watson, *Prewar Plans*, especially Chap. iii.

[2] Cline, *Washington Command Post*, p. 243, n. 18 for a vigorous defense of this independence by Col. W. W. Bessell, Jr., senior Army member of the JWPC.

[3] Ibid., p. 235.

Practically all communications with the theaters was maintained through the corresponding theater section in the Theater Group. Very early in the war the sections found it necessary to organize themselves along general staff lines in order to handle efficiently the various problems from the theaters and to coordinate them with the proper War Department staff and other agencies.[1]

The Navy Command Post

After Admiral King became Chief of Naval Operations (CNO) as well as Commander in Chief, U.S. Fleet (COMINCH) in March 1942, he retained the separate staffs of the two offices but reassigned some of their functions. Thenceforth strategic planning was conducted for the most part in the Plans Division of the Office of the Commander in Chief. The residual functions of the War Plans Division were eventually absorbed by the Logistics Plans Division, Office of the Chief of Naval Operations. The Chief of the Plans Division and his assistant were members of the JPS, and other officers of the Division were members of the JWPC. Responsibility for administration in the Navy was decentralized more than in the Army but not for the strategic planning and control of operations of the Fleet. For strategic planning Admiral King relied heavily on Vice Admiral Charles M. Cooke, Jr., who was Assistant Chief of Staff, Plans, until the middle of 1943, then Deputy Chief of Staff, and, finally, Chief of Staff to COMINCH.

---

[1] Ibid., p. 139.

In all these positions he remained King's chief strategical adviser. The Office of the COMINCH was rather compact and served Admiral King much as OPD did General Marshall. Functions of the Office of the CNO and of the Bureaus were roughly analogous to the War Department General Staff outside OPD.

Strategic responsibility for the Pacific was assigned to the United States by agreement with the British. In the exercise of this responsibility the Army acted as executive agent for the JCS in the Southwest Pacific Area as did the Navy in the Pacific Ocean Areas of Admiral Nimitz. Therefore OPD and the office of COMINCH continued to have special responsibilities in the planning and direction of operations in that vast theater. But there was a great interdependence of operations throughout the Pacific and both services were vitally con-concerned with the whole theater; neither could focus its attention too sharply on only one part of it.

Organizing the Pacific

ABDACOM and After

President Roosevelt attempted very early to work out a coordinated strategy in the Pacific with Russia, China, and Britain but achieved only limited success. In the end Stalin declined all invitations, and coordination with Chiang Kai-shek was limited to the China Theater. An Allied command was established, however, to defend the area of the

---

1
    Ltr, Adm Cook to Col Hoover, Acting Ch. Mil. Hist., 14 Aug 59, filed in OCMH.

Philippines, Malaya, and the East Indies. The area was called ABDA after the names of the four powers concerned -- Australian, British, Dutch, American -- and was placed under the command of General Sir Archibald P. Wavell, until then the British Commander-in-Chief, India. Beset with overwhelming difficulties from the first, ABDACOM was short-lived. One position after another fell to the Japanese: Singapore on 15 February and, finally, Java, where the Dutch surrendered their remaining forces on the 9th of March.

Loss of the Malay Barrier[1] effectively split the Allied forces in the Pacific from those in the Indian Ocean. Because of this and in recognition of each other's primary political interests and military capabilities, the American and British governments agreed to assign strategic responsibility of the Indian Ocean, including the Malay Peninsula and Sumatra, to the British and the areas east of there to the United States. Partly in anticipation of this, but for additional reasons as well, General Wavell was ordered back to India and General MacArthur was ordered to Australia from the Philippines even before the fall of Java.[2] At his request, MacArthur was allowed to choose the "right moment" for his departure from Luzon. That moment came on the 11th of March. He arrived in Australia on the 17th.

---

[1] Consisting of the Malay Peninsula, Sumatra, Java, and the islands stretching eastward to northwest Australia.

[2] Morton, Chap. x, pp. 5, 13. See also the Despatch by the Supreme Commander of the ABDA area to the CCS, 15 Jan 42 - 25 Feb 42, published by H. M. Stationery Office, 1948.

American Theater Commands

At the beginning of the war the United States had had four major commands in the Pacific, two army and two naval commands. Each service had one major headquarters located in Hawaii and one in the Philippines. The inadequacy of this organization in the face of the kind of war being fought was soon apparent. Unity of command was quickly established in Panama, under the Army, and in Hawaii, under the Navy, but not until the end of January was MacArthur given command of the small naval force then remaining in the Philippines.[1] These and other measures met the demands of the moment but they were only improvisations, piecemeal attacks on the problem of organizing this vast area into military commands.

After the dissolution of ABDACOM and the arrival of MacArthur in Australia, it was time for a more comprehensive look at the area and the problem of organizing it. As the army and navy planners undertook this task, many saw its objective as both obvious and the simple: the establishment of a unified joint command. General Marshall, especially, had pressed vigorously for this earlier. But there were too many service differences which could not be reconciled. The choice of commander, for example, seemed to lie between General MacArthur and Admiral Chester W. Nimitz, Commander in Chief, Pacific Fleet, but each was acceptable only by his own service. The problem went far beyond the difficulty of choosing a commander, but it was sufficient in itself

---

[1] Morton, Chap. vii, p. 29. Adm Hart had chosen to move the bulk of his fleet to the N.E.I.

to prevent the creation of one unified command, and it pretty well epitomized other disagreements over strategy, organization, and command relationships. In the face of this clear impasse, the planners quickly settled down to drawing a boundary line between two major Pacific theaters.

Everyone seemed to agree that there would be one predominently oceanic theater under the command of a naval officer and one theater incompassing the large land masses of the Southwest Pacific under an army officer. It was almost as easily agreed that the latter, with Australia at the core of it, would include areas north of Australia as far as Borneo and the Solomon Islands. Not agreed on were the Philippines, New Zealand, and the islands northeast of Australia, including the French island of New Caledonia and the New Hebrides and Fiji Islands. The Australians and New Zealanders, already disappointed in not having a voice in the JCS when Pacific matters were being considered, were insistent that the area of the two countries formed one strategic area and must not be separated.[1] This coincided with the views of the Army. But the Navy insisted that those areas east of Australia were an integral part of the line of communication from Hawaii and the West Coast of the United States. The defense of that line was the responsibility primarily of the Navy. Not long after Pearl Harbor Admiral King had told Admiral Nimitz that its defense was to have a priority only slightly below the defense of communications

---

[1] Morton, Chap. xi, p. 7.

to Hawaii.[1] In the end the Navy view prevailed. But in return the Philippines were included in the Southwest Pacific Area.

When General MacArthur assumed command of the Southwest Pacific Area (SWPA) on 18 April 1942 and Admiral Chester W. Nimitz of the Pacific Ocean Areas[2] (POA) on 8 May 1942, the basic organizational structure was established which would provide for the successful command of American and Allied forces in the Pacific for the next three years.

As Allied Commander in Chief, General MacArthur was barred from direct command of U.S. forces. Administrative control of the U.S. Army was vested in a subordinate headquarters, designated, at first, United States Army Forces in Australia (USAFIA). Operational control of all Allied forces was exercised through Allied Land Forces (ALF), Allied Air Forces (AAF), and Allied Naval Forces (ANF). The first was placed under the command of General Sir Thomas A. Blamey, Commander-in-Chief of the Australian Army. The last two were habitually under the command of an American.[3]

Admiral Nimitz, on the other hand, remained commander of the Pacific Fleet, directly subordinate to Admiral King in his capacity of Commander in Chief, U.S. Fleet. His area was divided into three

---

[1] Msg, COMINCH to CINCPAC 301740 Dec 41.

[2] First called, in the singular, Pacific Ocean Area. This term was a carry-over from ABC-1.

[3] The Campaigns of MacArthur in the Pacific, prepared by GHQ of the Supreme Commander of Allied Forces, Vol. I, pp. 31 - 33. Hereafter cited as SWPA History.

subareas -- North, Central, and South Pacific. Initially, he retained direct command of the first two while Vice Admiral Robert L. Ghormley was appointed commander of the last. It was in the South Pacific that the first counteroffensive would be launched and where operations would be most intimately related to those of MacArthur's forces.

The 30 March 1942 Directive

The original directives to the two area commanders, both dated 30 March 1942, assigned them essentially defensive missions.[1] In interpreting and implementing his directive, General MacArthur decided early to meet the enemy in New Guinea and to try to stop him there instead of waiting for him to move to Australia. The task was given to the New Guinea Force, predominantly Australian, under Allied Land Forces. In the execution of his directive from Nimitz, Admiral Ghormley gradually inched northward in occupying and garrisoning new positions, adding depth to the defense of his lines of communications.

Throughout the spring of 1942 long-ranging submarines and carrier and land based aircraft carried the war to the enemy. In April came the well-publicized Tokyo raid led by Lieutenant Colonel James H. Doolittle. But the Japanese were not yet ready to assume the defensive in the Pacific. In the Southwest Pacific they were preparing air bases in the southern Solomons and planned to take Port Moresby on the southern coast of Papua (the southeastern quarter of New Guinea). From these positions they could control much of the Coral

---

[1] The directives are reproduced in Appendices 3 and 4 of Morton, *Strategy and Command*.

Sea and dominate the approaches to a long stretch of the populated east coast of Australia. Later advances into the South Pacific -- the New Hebrides, New Caledonia, and the Fijis -- would effectively isolate Australia. In the Central and North Pacific they planned to seize Midway and the Western Aleutians simultaneously.[1] Attempts to carry out these plans resulted in two naval engagements which proved decisive in turning back the tide of Japanese victories in the Pacific.

The first was the Battle of the Coral Sea in early May. It was something of a draw as a purely naval battle, but it nevertheless thwarted the Japanese attempt to take Port Moresby from the sea just as General Blamey's forces later stopped their overland attempt at the Kakoda Pass. Midway, in early June, was a clear victory for the United States and changed the balance of naval power in the Pacific.[2]

The Counteroffensive

While the commanders were organizing their areas and performing their initial tasks under the 30 March directive, the planners in Washington began to plan the counteroffensive. For some time there had grown a general acceptance of the view that the route back to

---

[1] Japanese Monograph 45, Imperial General Headquarters Army High Command Record, prepared in Hq, FEC, pp. 48, 50 - 54. Hereafter cited as IGHQ.

[2] For complete accounts of these two naval battles see Samuel Eliot Morison, HISTORY OF THE UNITED STATES NAVAL OPERATIONS IN WORLD WAR II, Vol. IV, Coral Sea, Midway and Submarine Actions, May 1942 - August 1942 (Boston: Little, Brown and Company, 1950).

the Philippines started somewhere in the Solomon Sea area. The March directive to Nimitz was more explicit about this than was that to MacArthur. Nimitz was ordered to "prepare for the execution of major amphibious offensives against positions held by Japan, the initial offensives to be launched from the South Pacific Area and Southwest Pacific Area."[1]

MacArthur saw as his first major strategic objective, the area of the Bismark Sea. It constituted a major barrier to his advance back to the Philippines. In the shelter of its basin the Japanese were gathering strength for further advances to the South. Along the south shore was the Huon Peninsula stretching eastward from North-East New Guinea toward the big island of New Britain. At the north-eastern end of New Britain was Rabaul, the main Japanese base south of Truk. Its capture would provide the Allies with an excellent base with existing and potential facilities for air, ground, and naval forces. Other potential bases also existed around the littoral of the sea, for example, at Kavieng on New Ireland, on Manus Island in the Admiralties, and at Wewak in the North-East New Guinea.

Early in June, General MacArthur told General Marshall of his plan to recapture the strategic area of New Britain and New Ireland.[2] For this, however, he would need additions to his rather meager U.S.

---

[1] JCS Directive to CINCPOA, 30 Mar 42, cited above, p. . The wording of the directive was later to be used by the Navy as proof that the intent in March had been for the advance along this axis to be under the command of Nimitz.

[2] Plan TULSA. An abstract of TULSA II A, a Jul 42 revision is in OCMH files.

and Australian forces. The War Department planners quickly developed the idea into an outline plan culminating in the capture of Rabaul. At first the Navy planners agreed to these operations under the over-all command of General MacArthur. However, Admiral Cooke and Admiral King objected to both the strategy and the command arrangement. In the first place they objected to the excessive risk involved in moving such great distances through the relatively narrow and hostile waters of the Solomon Sea. Moreover, reasoned Admirals Cooke and King, the initial operations anywhere in the Pacific would be the primary responsibility of the Navy and the Marine Corps. All joint operations, therefore, should be under the command of Admiral Nimitz.

The 2 July 1942 Directive

After the presentation of several proposals and counter-proposals, General Marshall and Admiral King agreed upon a compromise. The initial operations in the southern Solomons (Guadalcanal and other nearby positions) of the South Pacific Area and of the South Pacific Forces. Thereafter amphibious forces would continue under the immediate command of the task force commander, but operations would be under over-all command of General MacArthur. This arrangement was confirmed by a directive to the theater commanders on 2 July 1942.[1]

The ultimate objective of operations provided for in the directive was the seizure of Rabaul and the control of the Bismark Sea. This

---
[1] A copy of the directive is reproduced in App. 5 of Morton, Strategy and Command. Background papers are filed in OPD 381 (SWPA), Case 80.

final task would be preceded by two others. Task One would be the seizure of the Southern Solomons (Guadalcanal was later selected as the first objective); and Task Two would involve the seizure of the rest of the Solomons and the Northeast Coast of New Guinea.

Guadalcanal and Buna

On 7 August a South Pacific task force landed the 1st Marine Division on Guadalcanal and the first major counterattack by American forces in World War II began. The next month New Guinea Force, having turned back the Japanese advance on Port Moresby began its descent of the Owen Stanley Mountains toward Buna. The Japanese offered stubborn resistance in both the Solomons and Papua. They were especially sensitive to the dangers of losing Guadalcanal and went to great lengths to sustain and even to reinforce themselves there. Nevertheless, both campaigns were virtually completed by the end of the year. The Japanese recognized the altered situation, and in a new operational plan of 31 December, Imperial General Headquarters directed the withdrawal of their forces from Guadalcanal and from Buna, yielding the offensive in those areas to the Allies.[1]

Theater Command and Strategy

The unexpectedly prolonged operations on Guadalcanal and the development of a critical shortage of shipping during the fall of

---

[1] IGHQ, p. 77. The Japanese Army-Navy Central Agreement (joint directive) is reproduced in App. 7 of Morton, Strategy and Command.

1942 reopened the question of strategy and command. As more and shorter steps up the Solomon chain appeared necessary and as the capture of Rabaul receded into the future, Admiral King again pressed for the continuation of the Solomon operations under command of Vice Admiral William F. Halsey, who, on 18 October had succeeded Admiral Ghormley as Commander, South Pacific Force. In this he was supported by Admiral Nimitz, but when, in February 1943, he suggested further that Nimitz and Halsey consider operations in the Gilbert and Ellice Islands, both officers objected. While recognizing the usefulness of such operations in securing the lines of communication to the Southwest Pacific and in diverting Japanese strength from the Solomons, Admiral Halsey felt that they would entail too great a dissipation of his forces and too great a logistical drain unless the attack in this direction were continued. And this he also opposed, for it would mean conducting difficult frontal attacks in a direction which did not lead to vital objectives. Rabaul, on the other hand, was an important center of Japan's system of defense in the Pacific. These views gave strong support to General MacArthur's constant and vigorous advocacy of a concentration of effort in the Pacific along the Southwest Pacific route back to the Philippines.

The 28 March 1943 Directive

In March 1943, a conference was convened in Washington, attended by representatives of the Pacific theaters, to discuss further strategy against Japan. Conflicting views were aired at length, but, in the end, the discussions reached then and following the conference reaffirmed all the essentials of the 2 July 1942 directive.[1] Ejection of the Japanese from the Aleutians would begin in May. Operations in the Central Pacific were postponed once more, and those in the South and Southwest Pacific were to continue under the strategic command of General MacArthur while Halsey would continue in direct command of operations in the Solomons. Moreover, after careful measurement of ends against means, modest increases were made in allocated menas, and, at the same time, more modest ends were assigned. The final objectives approved were short of Rabaul, and were simply to be positions from which the final assault on the Bismark Archipelago could be launched.

If Admiral King had favored a different strategy and had accepted only reluctantly the command arrangement, he was the champion among the Joint Chiefs for a greater allocation of means to the Pacific. With his insistent support, an increase in air and ground strength was alloted the Pacific at the expense of prior commitments to the United Kingdom. It was largely also at his insistence that operations against the Japanese in the Aleutians would begin in May.

New Urgency for Speed

Throughout the spring of 1943 there was a growing support among the various military planning agencies in Washington for a shift of

---

[1] The JCS directive of 28 March 43 is reproduced in App. 2, Morton, Strategy and Command.

the main effort to the Central Pacific. Concommitantly there grew a sense of urgency for speeding up operations in the war against Japan. One manifestation of this was a decision, over the protests of General MacArthur, to by-pass Rabaul and simply to neutralize it by air and naval blockade.

After finally acceding in March to the strategy and command set-up within the South-Southwest Pacific Areas, Admiral King had some new proposals in June. First he recommended that Central Pacific operations be started in the Marshalls about 1 November. This would curtail and slow down General MacArthur's operations and may have irrevocably shifted emphasis from the Southwest to the Central Pacific. At the same time he proposed making Admiral Nimitz responsible under the Joint Chiefs of Staff for timing major amphibious operations throughout the Pacific. This point of view was given strong support by the Joint Strategic Survey Committee which wanted an unequivocal decision in favor of the Central Pacific as the primary route of advance.

At the same time, General MacArthur was arguing strongly in favor of an advance to Mindanao, the southernmost of the large Philippine Islands. In urging an advance to Mindanao via New Guinea, he emphasized the importance of land-based aircraft in support of amphibious operations. Advance by other routes, he maintained, could be supported only by carrier-based aviation, and he pointed to the Japanese failure at Midway as an example of the danger of such operations. This was a powerful argument but unfortunately he chose a poor example to support it. Contrary to the widespread belief at that time, the Army's land-based aircraft had contributed very little to the victory at Midway.[1]

The preliminary opinion within the Joint War Plans Committee was something of a compromise of these two strategies. The JWPC recommended beginning the Central Pacific offensive but favored the primacy of this route of advance only slightly. The Committee saw the two routes as mutually supporting and as equally important. At the same time the members felt that it might become necessary to concentrate on one of the two routes or even a third in order to exploit developments which could not be predicted. The directive that went out to Nimitz on 20 July was essentially as recommended by the JWPC. With insufficient strength to go directly to the Marshalls and with the JCS unwilling to strengthen him at the expense of SWPA, Nimitz would have to secure positions in the Gilberts first.

CARTWHEEL

General MacArthur's representatives had come to the conference in March with a plan for recapturing Rabaul. The plan was called ELKTON II. But the directive which came out of the conference approved only the clearing of the Huon Peninsula, seizing of Western New Britain, and advancing in the Solomons into southern Bougainville. The planners in GHQ, SWPA fell to work at once revising the ELKTON Plan.

---

[1] Morison, *Coral Sea, Midway and Submarine Actions*, pp. 111, 159, n. 38; Craven and Cate, *Plans and Early Operations*, pp. 457 - 61.

A few days after the March directive was sent out to the Pacific, Admiral Halsey called on General MacArthur in Brisbane. It was the first meeting of the two men and the beginning of a most cordial personal relationship. Halsey easily achieved the main objective of his visit, which was to convince MacArthur of the need to secure intermediate objectives in the Central Solomons before moving to Bougainville.

When ELKTON III was completed, it provided for a series of closely coordinated operations over a period of about six months. The operations were known collectively by the code name CARTWHEEL.[1] In preparation for CARTWHEEL MacArthur and Halsey made a number of organizational changes in light of the lessons learned in the Guadalcanal and Papua campaigns, and they arranged for greater coordination and more effective mutual support in such fields as communications and intelligence.

After one delay CARTWHEEL began to roll on a broad front on 30 June. A powerful amphibious force under Vice Admiral Richmond Kelly Turner made its initial assault in the Central Solomons while a unit of the New Guinea Force made an unopposed landing at Nassau Bay just below Salamaua. Simultaneously, Lieutenant General Walter Kreuger's newly-formed ALAMO Force made unopposed landings in the Trobriand Islands in the Solomon Sea between the eastern and western flanks of CARTWHEEL.[2]

---

[1] John Miller, Jr., CARTWHEEL: The Reduction of Rabaul (Washington: U.S. Government Printing Office, 1960), for a complete account of these operations.

[2] ALAMO Force, virtually the same as Sixth U.S. Army, was directly under the control of GHQ, SWPA and not of Allied Land Forces.

At the end of 1943 the main objectives of CARTWHEEL had been achieved and the end was in sight. Most of the Huon Peninsula was in Allied hands, two landings had been made in Western New Britain, and in Bougainville fighter aircraft were already operating from air strips within the perimeter of the beachhead at Empress Augusta Bay. Although the campaign was not over until April 1944, MacArthur was already preparing to complete the encirclement of Rabaul and to proceed in the conquest of all New Guinea.

CARTWHEEL provided the forces of the Southwest Pacific their first experience with amphibious and airborne operations. Air, sea, and ground forces were combined in a remarkable variety of maneuvers which constantly bewildered, frustrated, and finally defeated the Japanese defenders. Surprise and flexibility also marked the operations in the Solomons. Despite the stubborn, even desperate resistance of the Japanese ground forces and the bold countermeasures of Admiral Koga, commander of the Japanese <u>Combined Fleet</u>, Admiral Halsey's forces took their objectives while at the same time inflicting great punishment on the enemy's air and naval forces.[1] Moreover, the parallel advances in the Solomons and up the New Guinea Coast were mutually supporting. Conducting them simultaneously paid great dividends in keeping the enemy off balance and in reducing his ability to concentrate his forces in protection of Rabaul.

---

[1] For an account of Admiral Koga's Operations <u>RO</u> see Morton, <u>Strategy and Command</u>, Chap. xxii, pp. 13 - 19.

Perhaps even more important was the support CARTWHEEL lent the operations in the Gilberts, which initiated the Central Pacific campaign in November. The cruiser and carrier strength of the <u>Combined Fleet</u> had been so weakened in fighting in the Solomons that Admiral Koga could not challenge the Central Pacific landings with his main striking force.

Starting the Central Pacific Advance

On the 20th of November Admiral Nimitz opened his Central Pacific offensive, which in less than two years would carry all the way to the Japanese homeland. Admiral Turner, recently released from the South Pacific, led his Northern Task Force against Makin while Rear Admiral Harry W. Hill's Southern Attack Force assaulted Tarawa. The 27th Infantry Division had a relatively easy task on Makin but the 2d Marine Division had an exceedingly difficult and costly job in reducing the much stronger defenses of Tarawa. In both cases it required but three days to secure the islands.[1]

These islands provided bases from which to support the next advance, into the Marshalls; and, in addition, the lessons learned there had a great influence on the future conduct of the war. Probably the most significant lesson was that it was feasible to mount such operations from distant bases and to secure local air superiority with carrier-based aircraft. If many had believed this in the past, here at last was proof.

---

[1] For a full account of these operations see Philip A. Crowl and Edmund G. Love, <u>Seizure of the Gilberts and Marshalls</u> (Washington: U.S. Government Printing Office, 1955).

In addition to these successes, the Aleutians were also recaptured during the summer. Attu was assaulted on 11 May and cleared after three weeks of hard fighting. Later, Shemya, and then Kiska were reoccupied without opposition.

By the end of the year, then, the wheel of fortune had made a full half turn. American military power was developing in the Pacific and closing inexorably on the Japanese' inner zone of defense. Still undetermined, though, was just how this power would ultimately be brought to bear against Japan in forcing her surrender to the will of the United Nations.

CHAPTER IV

THE LONG RANGE PLAN: COMMITMENT TO TOTAL WAR

Neither the ORANGE nor the RAINBOW Plans established a strategy and a long-range plan for the defeat of Japan. The time-honored objective was simply to establish in the Western Pacific naval strength superior to Japan. After that a blockade would ultimately force Japan to sue for peace. Details of strategy had been concerned solely with defense of American possessions in the Pacific, with the generation of military power within the "strategic triangle" of the Eastern Pacific, and then the projection of that power westward to the vicinity of the Philippines and (sometimes and vaguely) the China Coast. Operations beyond that were not developed in detail.

Strategic Concepts and Nascent Plans

Finally, on 4 April 1941, Admiral Stark and General Marshall asked the Administrator of Export Control to prepare a plan for conducting economic warfare against the Axis Powers.[1] The Administrator was then Brigadier General R. L. Maxwell. Committees of his agency, whose membership represented a large number of departments and separate executive agencies of government, had been engaged for some time in preparing studies on which a plan for economic warfare could be based.

---

[1] Jt. ltr from Stark and Marshall, 4 Apr 41, in WPD 4402-6.

Therefore, in the remarkably short time of 27 days, they were able to prepare a draft in two volumes of what was entitled a "Coordinated Plan of Economic Action in Relation to Japan."[1] While it never achieved the final form of an approved plan, it gave some meaning to the vague plans for a blockade of Japan and became an important guide to later actions against Japan, both before and after Pearl Harbor.

The Army had given even less thought than had the Navy to the final operations necessary to defeat Japan. Occasionally in ORANGE planning there had been vague hints about taking "such further actions as may be required" if the isolation of Japan and the crippling of her economic life failed to force her surrender.[2] Sometimes, too, there were a few cautious words about possible land operations in China. But it is unlikely that many Army officers other than Air Corps officers had much faith in any strategy short of defeating the Japanese Army in Japan. However, an army that had little hope even for a successful defense of the Philippines could not give much thought to offensive land operations against Japan.

The Army Air Corps between the World Wars gradually evolved a doctrine of air power which was essentially and primarily offensive.[3] Enthusiastic advocates of a greater reliance on air power claimed repeatedly that the older services were so imbued with the idea that

---

[1] A copy, dated 1 May 41, is in the files of OCMH.

[2] Supra, p.

[3] For an excellent discussion of this development, see Craven and Cate, Plans and Early Operations, esp. pp. 33 - 54.

the foremost objective of all military operations was the destruction of the enemy fleet and of his armies in the field that they had forgotten the ultimate objective of war, namely, the imposition of one's will on that of the enemy nation. This could best be accomplished by direct attack upon vital objectives in the enemy nation's "economic structure."

Aircraft available or planned before World War II could not strike across oceans, but airmen were not unmindful of the possibilities of using bases of allies within flying distance of potential enemies. In 1937 the Commanding General of GHQ Air Force wrote: "With landing fields at Wake and Guam [the B-17] could fly to the Philippines and Asia. However, our National Policy is defensive, and we cannot now consider such possibilities."[1]

In 1935 the Joint Board had assigned certain missions to army aviation in addition to direct support of army combat operations. These included the conduct of "air operations over the sea in direct defense of the coast" and, under certain conditions, the conduct of "air operations in support of or *in lieu* of naval forces."[2]

It was natural enough, then, that the air planners should have begun thinking very early in the war about bringing air power directly to bear against the Japanese homeland. Almost immediately after Pearl Harbor the United States undertook to secure air bases in Siberia

---

[1] Ltr cited by Craven and Cate, *Early Plans and Operations*, pp. 68 - 69.

[2] Joint Action of Army and Navy, a 1935 policy statement cited by Craven and Cate, p. 48. Emphasis added.

from which to bomb Japan.[1] But these efforts came to naught. At ARCADIA there was a brief and inconclusive discussion of the possibility of sending no fewer than 50 heavy bombers to China to bomb Japan.[2] Brigadier General Simon B. Buckner and Captain Ralph C. Parker, Army and Navy commanders in Alaska submitted a plan shortly after Pearl Harbor for mounting an offensive from Alaska and the Aleutians. But the failure to reach agreement with Russia on the Siberian bases and the great demands elsewhere for resources, especially aircraft, forced General Marshall and Admiral King to disapprove the plan at that time.[3]

The First Long-Range Plan

The Navy was prepared very early to seize bases in the Ellice Islands and New Hebrides in preparation for future offensives into the Solomons. But the Army could not spare the ground and air forces for garrisons nor the shipping to sustain them. After Coral Sea in May, however, Army planners could afford to look more confidently toward the future. On 31 May Brigadier General Thomas T. Handy recommended to the other members of the JPS that the JUSSC be directed to prepare "plans for an offensive leading to the defeat of Japan." In preparing these plans they would be asked to consider the "national

---

[1] For a discussion of these planning activities, see Matloff and Snell, *Strategic Planning, 1941-1942*, pp. 142 - 46.

[2] Ibid., p. 139, n. 37.

[3] WPD memorandum for the Chief of Staff, 13 Mar 43, sub: Joint Army-Navy Plan for Alaska. OPD 381 Alaska, Case 6.

objectives" of the United States and to recommend whether a limited or an unlimited war should be planned against Japan. A limited war he described briefly as one designed to strangle Japan economically through destroying her external lines of communication. By an unlimited war he meant the seizure and occupation of one or more of the four main home islands.[1] What the senior planners would ask, in effect, was whether Japan could be defeated short of invasion. It was the basic question of the war. It would not be faced squarely for another year and would not be answered unequivocally for three years. Until there was an answer, it would be impossible to settle on a firm concept and a definitive plan for defeating Japan. It was clearly too early to expect an answer. It was even too early to begin a deliberate search for the answer. Too many questions of global strategy remained unanswered.

General Marshall and Admiral King went to London less than two months later to discuss global strategy. From the instructions to the two officers it was clear that the most urgent strategic problem was the prevention of the collapse of Russia.[2] The two Allies were inclined to take desperate measures to prevent that. However, the Combined Chiefs also discussed possible courses of action to be taken in the event of Russia's collapse. One possible course considered

---

[1] Memo, Brig Gen Handy for Adm Turner and Col Craig, 31 May 42, no sub, in ABC Japan (8-27-42), Sec. 1.

[2] A copy of the memo to Gen Marshall and Adm King, sub: Instructions for London Conference, July 1942, 15 Jul 42 is reproduced in App. B of Matloff and Snell, *Strategic Planning, 1941-1942*.

was an all-out effort in the Pacific.

The study of the problem of what to do in the event of Russia's collapse was already underway in Washington.[1] One of the planners' conclusions was that a strategic plan for the defeat of Japan should be prepared to meet those conditions. This recommendation was accepted and enlarged on. The planners were directed to consider not merely the consequences of a Russian collapse but to prepare an over-all plan for the defeat of Japan in any foreseeable circumstance.[2] Study of the problem continued through the next few months and had produced no more than a strategic estimate of the situation by the time of the Casablanca Conference in January 1943.

Known sometimes by the code word ANFA, this was the first mid-war strategy conference between Churchill and Roosevelt and their military chiefs.[3] No change was made there in the basic Europe-first strategy, but the possibility of a large-scale invasion of the Continent during 1943 was virtually written off by the military leaders. The British urged greater commitment of available forces to the Mediterranean in 1943 while the Americans were insistent upon maintaining pressure on the Japanese, both in the Pacific and in the China-Burma-India Theater.

---

[1] J.P.S. 43, "Strategic Policy of the United Nations and the United States on the Collapse of Russia," 7 Aug 42. In the covering "Note by the Secretaries," it was stated that the study had been undertaken in compliance with a directive from Gen Eisenhower and Admiral Turner. Since these two were members of the old Joint Board's Joint Planning Committee, this must have been about the last important planning directive from that body. A cy of J.P.S. 43 is in ABC 384 USSR (6-1-42).

[2] Mins, JPS 29th Mtg, 19 Aug 42, Item 4.

[3] For an account of the conference, see Maurice Matloff, <u>Strategic Planning for Coalition Warfare, 1943-1944</u> (Washington: U.S. Government Printing Office, 1959), pp. 18 - 42.

The result was a compromise. In the Pacific, offensives would continue in both the Central and Southwest Areas; in the Mediterranean, offensives would continue against Italy.

The most significant event at the conference was the announcement of the unconditional surrender formula. Its influence on the conduct of World War II will surely be debated as long as that war is studied. Strict adherence to it, it seems plain enough in retrospect, meant a commitment to total and unlimited war.

During the next few weeks the JUSSC resumed their study of Pacific strategy and reported their findings on 15 February 1943.[1] Rear Admiral B. H. Bieri, navy member of the JPS criticized their report as no more than an analysis of the Casablanca Conference. What was needed was a plan of operations which would follow the defeat of Germany. At his recommendation a new directive was given the JUSSC to continue the preparation of a broad strategic plan for the defeat of Japan.[2]

Before it could complete its task the JUSSC was succeeded by a new body, the JWPC, as a result of a reorganization of the JCS. It submitted its incomplete plan on 28 April 1943.[3] This plan, although

---

[1] JPS 67/3, "Operations in the South and Southwest Pacific Areas during 1943," 15 Feb 43, in ABC 381 (8-27-42), Sec. I.

[2] Mins, JPS 61st Mtg, 24 Feb 43, Item 4.

[3] JPS 67/4, Rpt by JUSSC, "Strategic Plan for the Defeat of Japan," 28 Apr 43, in ABC 381 (8-27-42), Sec. I. Memo, Jt. Secys JWPC to JPS, "Strategic Plan for the Defeat of Japan," 27 Apr 43, in CCS 381 Japan (8-25-42), Sec. 2.

it was entitled "Strategic Plan for the Defeat of Japan," was still more a concept than a plan. Yet it is a landmark in the evolution of Pacific strategy. In the first place, the possibility of an invasion of Japan was faced squarely. Still, the planners were hopeful that a tight naval blockade or a sustained aerial bombardment might force Japan's surrender. Any such final aerial assault would have to be delivered from China, they thought, but since the Burma Road would never have a sufficient capacity to support such operations, another route into China would have to be opened. Hong Kong was selected as the preferred point of entry from the sea. The best route from the United States to Hong Kong would be from the Central Pacific through the Celebes, Sulu, and the South China Seas. The best route from the United Kingdom lay through the Malacca Straits and the South China Sea.

This plan was neither accepted nor rejected but was drawn upon heavily by the new JWPC in completing a plan which it presented a few days later for use by the JCS at the forthcoming TRIDENT Conference.[1] The new plan placed more emphasis on potentialities of naval blockade as an alternative to invasion. There was not even a suggestion that aerial bombardment alone might force Japan to surrender. Perhaps the most important change was the recommendation that the advance to Hong Kong from the Pacific be made from both the Central and Southwest

---

[1] Held in May in Washington. See Matloff, Strategic Planning, 1943-1944, pp. 126 - 145.

Pacific areas. The last change apparently resulted from an objection of Captain C. W. Moore, USN, that the advantages of using both routes had not been considered in the JUSSC plan. The mutual support of the two routes and the greater flexibility possible through the wider choice of successive objectives were arguments frequently used thereafter, especially by American spokesmen and planners in dealing with the British. Thus, by the time of TRIDENT all the major concepts of how to achieve victory in the Pacific and which were to be debated during the war existed in at least embryonic form. Also, the other major problems standing in the way of final decisions of strategy were beginning to be recognized for what they were. Now the planners would come to grips with them.

The Major Strategic Factors

As shown by General Handy's memorandum of a year before, the alternative to invasion was then seen to be "strangulation," essentially a naval task. This could be achieved by destroying Japan's naval and merchant shipping through attacks from below, from above, and from the surface of the sea and by disrupting her lines of communication through amphibious and aerial assaults. It was only later and only gradually that strategic aerial bombardment of the Japanese homeland became widely accepted as another strategic method of defeating Japan, a method clearly distinguishable from invasion and blockade. It was not at all a new concept to the followers and heirs of Mitchell and Douhet, and its advocates counted on two effects of aerial bombardment to bring Japan to her knees -- shock and destruction. Massive attacks of high explosive and incendiary bombs would destroy the enemy's means of resistance and the shock of such attacks would destroy his will to resist. Opinions often cut across service lines, but essentially, the three concepts of the ultimate defeat of Japan were held respectively by officers of the Army, the Navy, and the Air Forces.[1] Planners favored one and then another of the three, but circumstances allowed a continual deferment of a final decision. An unequivocal choice among them was not made until just before the end of the war.

An only slightly less fundamental problem lay in the choice of the route along which the main attack would be directed toward Japan. There were five principal choices, each with possible variations. One was the so-called Northern Route. Although there was almost a land bridge from Alaska to Siberia via the Seward Peninsula and Bering Strait, the only feasible route lay across the Aleutian chain to Paramushiru in the northern Kuriles (preferably via the Kamchatka Peninsula), and thence south to Hokkaido. The Joint Planners concluded very early that the success of such an advance required the cooperation of Russia.[2] Bases in Siberia would be the first requirement.

---

[1] I sometimes use the title "Air Force" for convenience and simplicity. It should be borne in mind, however, that the United States Air Force did not exist until 1947. It is a direct descendent of the United States Army Air Forces of World War II, the nucleus of which was the Army Air Corps.

[2] *Supra*, p.   . It was the consideration of these problems which triggered the search for a long-range plan.

In addition Russia could furnish valuable intelligence information. Best of all, she could conduct coordinated attacks from her Maritime Provinces and from Northern Sakhalin. This route led to the invasion of at least one of the main home islands of Japan and so did not appeal strongly to proponents of the blockade and bombardment concepts. In addition, its successful use depended heavily upon the cooperation of a difficult ally.

A second route led across the Central Pacific, generally as envisaged by the pre-war ORANGE Plan. The ORANGE Plan was not so much a plan for the defeat of Japan as simply a plan for the recapture of the Philippines while concurrently developing a naval blockade of Japan. Yet very early in the war the advocates of this route of advance began to doubt whether it was really necessary to reenter the Philippines in order to defeat Japan. Any advance across the Central Pacific had some clear advantages. Although it would mean the pursuit of a predominantly naval strategy, it held promise also of securing bases from which very long range bombardment of Japan could be conducted. The war in Europe was primarily a land and air war and had first call on Allied army and air forces. Also, the bulk of the British Fleet was deployed in that theater, thereby greatly reducing the need there for American naval power. Therefore, the growing might of the U.S. Navy could best be exploited in the Pacific, especially the Central Pacific. Moreover, the pursuance of this strategy and the use of this route freed the United States' effort of any important dependence upon Allied assistance -- or interference.

A third route was from the south. It led almost unavoidably through the Philippines whether the core of the thrust were through New Guinea or through islands west or east of New Guinea. Its use would require larger land forces for extensive ground combat, and it led to areas suitable for staging the massive forces necessary for the invasion of Japan. Advance along this line would also cut off Japan's communication with its rich conquests of Southeast Asia and would yield bases from which strategic bombardment of targets in Southeast Asia and, later, of targets in the Japanese homeland could be conducted. Use of this route entailed the coordination of U.S. strategy and forces with those of several allies. Cooperation with Australia and New Zealand, the two principal allies, was easy, as those two countries found that the subordination of their war effort to the leadership of the United States served their interests quite satisfactorily. Dutch contributions, after the fall of the Indies, and the French, except for bases in New Caledonia, were not significant.

A fourth route led overland through China to the coast of the South and East China Seas. Success along this route would have several desirable by-products, such as the containment of large Japanese forces and the capture of naval bases and of suitable staging areas for invasion forces, but its most important objective would be in securing air bases for the strategic bombardment of Japan. Its success, however, depended upon the defensive power of the Chinese forces of Chaing Kai-shek. These forces were limited in their offensive capability and required logistical support which could be brought in only by an overland route through Burma until such time as a Chinese sea port were opened up. Responsibility for opening such an overland route belonged largely to the British. Success here, then, was impossible without great effort on the part of two allies of the United States.

A fifth route lay through the Malacca Strait (between Sumatra and Malaya) or, alternatively, through the Soenda Strait (between Sumatra and Java) and up the western shore of the South China Sea. Responsibility for opening such a route would be almost entirely British. It perhaps should not be included as a separate route, as it could never be expected to develop enough momentum to carry all the way to Japan but would converge in the vicinity of Hong Kong with other routes. Still, it was a route which received serious consideration from time to time.

Divided opinions existed in other areas of strategic planning, also. Cleavages often cut across service lines and were frequently drawn more along lines dividing theaters and areas of operations. For example, timing of operations inevitably involved priority of one area of operation over another and, thus, was a constant problem of choice and decision. On the other hand, personality conflicts were often reinforced by service loyalties. General MacArthur was the transcendent example. The Navy early and firmly refused to accept General MacArthur as the supreme commander for the Pacific Theater; the Army likewise was not willing to place the Southwest Pacific Area under the command of a naval officer.

Combined Decisions and Plans -- TRIDENT to QUADRANT

In the face of these and other unresolved differences of opinion, the strategy employed against Japan remained flexible and opportunistic. By the time of the TRIDENT Conference, some concensus did exist, however, at least among the U.S. planners, and it was then time for them to face the views of the British and to seek resolution and compromise of Allied differences before U.S. views were firm. Future strategy would develop not willy-nilly, exactly, but in a kind of negative fashion, resulting more from a gradual elimination of possibilities than from a positive growth of new strategic plans and concepts.

The TRIDENT decisions contributed nothing of substance to the long-range plan for the defeat of Japan. The official statement of the conference confirmed once again the priority of effort against the European Axis while concurrently "maintain[ing] and extend[ing] unremitting pressure against JAPAN with the purpose of continually reducing her military power and attaining positions from which her ultimate surrender can be forced."[1] In support of this, specific

---

[1] See Morton, *Strategy and Command*, Chap. xxiii, pp. 1 - 10 for an account of the conference.

operations in the Pacific for 1943-44 were approved. Dates, except for the immediate operations, were not definite, but the objectives themselves were much more definite than those approved at Casablanca. They included Rabaul, advances in the Central Pacific as far as the Carolines, and ejection of the Japanese from the Aleutians. Commitment to these operations was a triumph for the Americans. The British, as always, were fearful of too great a drain on Allied resources on operations outside the European area; and the Americans were just as fearful of the consequences of allowing Japan to consolidate her conquests and strengthen her defenses. The American people, General Marshall asserted, would not tolerate delay in prosecuting the Pacific War.[1]

In the view of the British, the American plan presented at TRIDENT was not sufficiently definite. At the last meeting of the conference, therefore, the CCS directed that further work be done on it. The directive was for a U.S. planning team to visit London and later for a British team to visit Washington and together to "prepare for consideration by the Combined Chiefs of Staff an appreciation leading to an outline plan for the defeat of Japan including an estimate of the forces required for its implementation."[2]

As the American and British planners met, first in London, then in Washington during the summer, divergencies of view became more

---

[1] Min, 83d mtg, CCS, 13 May 43.
[2] Min, CCS 90th mtg, 24 May 43, Item 3. The U.S. team was the Red Team of the JWPC.

and more apparent. Still, they were able to complete an appreciation and plan before the QUADRANT Conference convened at Quebec in August. On 9 August, the day after it was turned over to the Combined Staff Planners, the U.S. planning team -- Captain H. B. Slocum, USN, Colonel E. H. McDaniel, USA, and Colonel W. R. Wolfinbarger, USA -- summarized for the American planners and delegates these differences.[1] The differences were not always clear in the plan itself, which represented a compromise of views. The source of most disagreement was the different evaluation of direct assistance to China. The British continued to minimize the fighting potential of the Chinese forces, and this attitude re-enforced their aversion to the jungle fighting in Burma, which was aimed directly at sustaining the Chinese. While they agreed to the importance of Hong Kong as a base for further operations against Japan, they were not eager for it to be captured by the Chinese. Their preferred route was via Singapore, the Malacca Strait and the coast of Indo China. But beyond this, all operations against the Japanese assumed an importance far below those against the European Axis. It was apparent, in fact, that the British did not even want to discuss the Pacific and Asiatic theaters at QUADRANT.[2]

---

[1] Memo, Capt Slocum, et al., for Joint Staff Planners, 9 Aug 43, sub: Strategic Plan for the Defeat of Japan, OPD 381 Security, Case 192.

[2] The British urged that the plan be completed at Quebec for later consideration by the Combined Chiefs of Staff. The 8 Aug plan (C.P.S. 83, "Appreciation and Plan for the Defeat of Japan") and background papers are filed in ABC 381 Japan (27 Aug 42), Sec. 3.

The British failed to realize this desire, for the very first order of business at QUADRANT was the 8 August plan. It began with an interesting appraisal of Japanese psychology. Japan had never been invaded, the planners pointed out. Moreover, the tenaciousness of her soldiers in battle and the stoicism of her people in the face of adversity were remarkable. In light of these considerations, the Allied objective of unconditional surrender might require new expression as a military objective. The destruction of Japan's capacity to resist and not simply her will to resist was perhaps a better way to express the military objective. How then to achieve this destruction became the central problem.

Japan might be forced to surrender before her homeland was invaded, but it would be dangerous to count on this, and any plan for the defeat of Japan should provide for invasion. Unlike the JWPC plan submitted at TRIDENT (May 1943), which stressed the strategy of naval blockade as an alternative to invasion, this plan looked more hopefully at the potentiality of aerial bombardment as had the last JUSSC plan (April 1943). Perhaps the planners felt that the basic and vital role of naval power in such an oceanic area was too obvious to require elaboration, but the fact is that the purely naval aspects of the plan were passed over rather lightly, and the possibility of forcing Japan's surrender through a strategy of naval blockade was not even expressed. Happily, the logical pursuit of the bombardment strategy, even if it failed alone to force Japan's surrender, would achieve the very conditions necessary and preliminary to invasion anyway. Such a strategy would require an increasing number of bases in ever closer proximity to the enemy homeland. These bases could be used for staging the invasion forces. The bombardment would reduce the enemy's will and capability for resistance sufficiently to ensure the success of the invasion.

The planners thought that the best area for these bases could be found in the Shanghai area, but the likelihood of securing this area at a reasonably early date was not good. Hong Kong, Formosa, and Luzon would be acceptable in that order as substitutes. And failing this, Hainan augmented by bases in the Ryukyus would do. The northern littoral of the South China Sea, then, was established as the primary intermediate objective short of Japan itself.

Having established the objective area, the planners once again examined the various possible approaches to it -- overland across China, up from the Indies via the Malacca or the Soenda Straits, along the New Guinea-Philippines axis from the South-Southwest Pacific, and straight across the Pacific through the Mandates. Another approach, from the north, leading toward another possible major intermediate objective in the Kuriles or Hokkaido was examined separately. All these approaches had some merit and might be used as developing circumstances permitted, but the principal effort would be made from the Central Pacific. United Nations forces should stand ready to take advantage of any unexpected opportunities, the planners conceded, but, failing such altered circumstances, all other efforts should be held subsidiary to the main effort through the Mandates.

The planners deliberately eschewed optimism, and their timetable provided for reaching the great intermediate objective area no later than (and, thus, perhaps as late as) the end of 1946. Final operations would then run into 1947 and perhaps 1948. The undesirability of such prolonged operations was obvious to all. Without being very specific, the planners recognized the need for finding short cuts. One such possible short cut lay in the maximum exploitation of superior and growing air power. Another possible short cut lay in a deliberate policy of by-passing areas which would involve extensive land campaigns to capture. Proper use of superior air and naval power should make this tactic possible. It would have a bonus advantage, too; for the support of their by-passed and isolated garrisons would be a further drain on the weakening Japanese air and naval forces.

In that portion of the plan concerning the invasion there were at least two important and categorical conclusions. One was that to insure the defeat of Japan, the United States must be prepared to invade. Second, the main objective of an invasion should be the Tokyo-Yokohama area, the political and industrial heart of the nation. It was too early to determine whether an assault directly upon the Tokyo Plain or anywhere on the island of Honshu from distant bases were feasible. Certain advantages and disadvantages of landing first on one of the other three main islands were discussed. In any case certain minimum conditions had to obtain before the invasion could be undertaken. In simplest terms these included, first, the maximum reduction of Japanese powers of resistance, and, second, the securing of advance bases for the invasion forces. Bases within no more than 2,000 miles were needed for naval units, especially for smaller ships. Bases for embarking the large land forces also could be no farther away than this. Minimum requirements for bases could be met in either of four areas: (1) the Aleutians and the Alaska Peninsula, (2) the Carolines and the Marshalls, (3) South Philippines and North Borneo, or (4) Indo-China and Singapore.

Closer bases, from 500 to 700 miles from the objective area, would be needed for basing landing craft to be used for ferrying men and vehicles in the ship-to-shore assault. Airfields for troop-carrier aircraft and for replacement aircraft for the fleet would be needed within the same ranges. If the Shanghai area could not be seized, bases in the Ryukyus, the Bonins, or the Kuriles could partially fill these needs, but they could not furnish sufficient facilities for troop-carrier aircraft. The planners were hopeful that aircraft carriers or flying boats would be developed to meet this problem. The planners briefly considered conducting a shore-to-shore assault against Japan but concluded that securing bases for such operations would require an effort comparable to that for the invasion of Japan itself.

To a very large extent, the two principal conditions that had to be satisfied prior to invasion — reduction of Japan's power of resistance and the capture of advance bases — amounted to the same thing. In the process of capturing bases on or near the China coast and of securing the lines of communications to them the Allies would interrupt Japan's communications and would destroy much of her military power.

There were a number of areas in which a bomber offensive against Japan could be based. The planners considered in turn the islands outlying Japan, areas in Siberia, Manchuria, Korea, Japan itself (Hokkaido), Formosa, the Philippines, and China, and even the open sea (aircraft carriers). They concluded that plans should be based on the use of China or Formosa or both, augmented by attacks from aircraft carriers. As for fighter and tactical bomber bases, the Allies would "have to rely almost entirely on carrier-borne air support for the invasion of Japan." In fact they stated that the "increased use of this type of support offer/ed/ the most hopeful prospect of accelerating the date by which we /could/ undertake the invasion."[1]

The planners saw great value in China's remaining in the war. She was not only containing approximately 20% of the Japanese ground forces, but she also could provide territory which would almost certainly be needed for mounting the final air and naval offensives and for staging at least a part of the forces needed in an invasion. Moreover, the American planners viewed more optimistically than did the British the potential offensive capability of the Chinese Army, providing it received sufficient logistic support, equipment, and training

---

[1] P. 23 of the plan.

assistance. They viewed the battle for China as a combination of overland and amphibious operations. The projected timing of these operations was vague but they were foreseen as long and drawn out. The planners estimated that even after the capture of Hong Kong another eighteen months to two years would pass before enough supplies could be brought in to support ten U.S. or British divisions and sufficient air forces (784 bombers and 716 supporting aircraft) to conduct a strategic bombing offensive.

In forwarding the plan to the Combined Chiefs of Staff, the Combined Staff Planners agreed with much of it but felt that it provided for too long a war. Japan had won most of her objectives, they said; and failure to reverse this situation before 1947 would seriously hazard the United Nations' chance of ever reversing it.[1] They therefore recommended that the redeployment of forces from Europe to the Pacific begin four to six months before the predicted surrender of Germany. The Americans urged that, for planning purposes, the target date for the defeat of Japan be fixed at twelve months after Germany's surrender.[2] The British, also, were anxious to find a way to shorten the war but argued that such an early target date could not be met without a premature invasion of Japan, one launched

---

[1] Memo, CPS for CCS, sub: Comments on the Strategic Plan for the Defeat of Japan, 16 Aug 43, in ABC 381 Japan (27 Aug 42), Sec. 3.

[2] Inspiration of this idea apparently came from the U.S. Navy. On 6 May 43 Adm Cooke proposed this in a memo to Adm King. Copy furnished by Adm Cooke is on file in OCMH.

before blockade and bombardment had sufficiently softened up the Japanese home islands. Their objection must have had a familiar ring to those who had long advocated an early attack across the English Channel.

The Americans also disagreed with the relative importance assigned the routes of advance in the Pacific. They considered the Central and South-Southwest Pacific routes as mutually supporting and co-ordinate, at least in the current phase of the war. The British thought the former promised faster progress and less expense in men and materiel. Also a variety of differences existed over the strategy to be followed in Southeast Asia. The British wanted to give higher priority to recapturing Singapore and to reopening a sea route through the Malacca Straits at the expense of the effort to clear Burma. This operation especially interested Prime Minister Churchill, who compared it to the Dardenelles in 1915.

The Air Plan for the Defeat of Japan

As a possible test for the feasibility of defeating Japan within twelve months after the defeat of Germany, the U.S.A.A.F. was asked to prepare a plan to meet this target date. It was drawn up in a hurry and was presented before the Quebec Conference ended.[1] A generally sympathetic atmosphere prevailed, providing a propitious time

---

[1] The plan (C.C.S. 323, "Air Plan for the Defeat of Japan," 20 Aug 43) and some related papers are in ABC 381 Japan (23 Aug 42), Sec. 3.

for presenting such a plan. A great sense of urgency had developed for getting on with the war in the Pacific.

The plan provided for an aerial offensive against Japan which would so destroy her ability to resist as to allow occupation of the home islands by the fall of 1945, i.e., within 12 months of the assumed defeat of Germany. By an engenious method of planning, it was calculated that approximately 130,000 tons of bombs would reduce Japan to virtual helplessness. It was further calculated that one group of B-29 bombers in China could average delivering 700 tons of bombs per month. It therefore would require 186 group-months to deliver the total amount of destruction. Beginning with 4 groups of B-29's in June 1944, the plan called for a gradual build-up until 20 groups would finally be operating from forward bases in China by May 1945. The accumulated delivery of bombs during the 11 months of build-up and the following 3 months would equal the required 130,000 tons by July 1945.[1] The area of the bases centered on Changsha, an area formed by an arc with a 1,500 mile radius (practical radius of a B-29) drawn from the center of Japan's main industrial area and by an arc with an 800 mile radius (practical radius of supporting transport aircraft) drawn from Kunming (center of the staging area furnishing

---

[1] According to U.S. Strategic Bombing Survey, Summary Report (Pacific War), (Washington: U.S. Government Printing Office, 1946), p. 16, B-29's dropped a total of 147,000 tons of bombs on the Japanese home islands. This is the equivalent of 210 group-months of operation, figuring 28 airplanes per group, five group missions per month, ten tons of bombs per sortie, and with groups on a 50% operational basis.

logistical support for the Changsha area). The base area for the logistical support would be another 800 miles to the rear of Kunming and centered around Calcutta.

In addition, two groups of B-29's were to operate from the Aleutians against Hokkaido. The target area for the China-based groups, however, would stretch from Nagasaki to Tokyo and would include 75% of the selected strategic targets in Japan.

The Combined Chiefs recognized the plan as bold and imaginative but criticized its failure to consider adequately either the difficulty of supporting it logistically or the effect it might have on Overlord. Apparently no shipping or logistics planners had been called upon for guidance. It therefore directed the Combined Staff Planners to study the plan for further feasibility. After further study in Washington and by commanders in India, China, and the Aleutians, the planners concluded that the basic concept of using heavy bombers for transports from India to China was sound and that further study of this capability should be made and the results included in the Strategic Plan for the Defeat of Japan. However, a recalculation of B-24's (converted to transports) required by the plan revealed that a much greater number would be required than could be provided.[1]

Combined Decisions and Plans -- QUADRANT to SEXTANT

The Combined Chiefs of Staff did not find either the over-all plan or the air plan satisfactory. They directed their planners to

---

[1] This report is J.P.S. 271, "Studies on the Defeat of Japan," 11 Sep 43, in ABC 381 Japan (27 Aug 42), Sec. 3.

restudy the first and to revise it to provide for the defeat of Japan twelve months after Germany's defeat. The air plan was dropped but the planners were directed to investigate the extent to which air attacks could be brought to bear on Japan.[1]

The October Plan

The new plan was completed by late October.[2] The combined planners had now concluded that invasion was necessary in order to force Japan's unconditional surrender, at least if it were to be forced at a reasonably early date. Even so, invasion and defeat of Japan by the fall of 1945, appeared unlikely. The most optimistic possibilities they could visualize were presented as four courses of action. First was the invasion of Hokkaido by coming straight in from the Pacific in the summer of 1945. Second was the invasion of Formosa from the Pacific in the spring of 1945. Third was the capture of Singapore by the end of 1945 followed by invasion of Formosa from both the Pacific and the South China Seas in the winter of 1945-46. Fourth was similar to the third, consisting of a diversion in Southeast Asia in the spring of 1945 followed by the capture of Formosa from the Pacific in the winter of 1945-46. Although the first choice came nearer to satisfying the CCS directive, the planners recommended the second choice as the "most promising way of finishing the war

---

[1] ABC 334 (1-23-42), Sec. 5. Mins, CCS 119th mtg, 17 Sep 43, Item 10.

[2] C.P.S. 86/2, "The Defeat of Japan Within Twelve Months After the Defeat of Germany," 25 Oct 43, in ABC 381 Japan (8-27-42), Sec. 5.

comparatively soon" with acceptable risks. In support of this strategy they offered a schedule of operations culminating in an invasion of Hokkaido in the summer of 1946 and of Honshu in the fall.

While this schedule was the most optimistic the planners considered safe to count on, a number of possible favorable developments would allow a speed-up. The final schedule would depend upon the speed of current and planned operations in the Southwest and Central Pacific and upon the effectiveness of U.S. submarines against Japanese shipping. By-passing Truk in a more direct drive on the Marianas would be especially helpful. Attacks against Japan by carrier-based aircraft and by B-29's were still untried methods and their effect on the timetable was unknown. And, finally, the extent and effectiveness of Soviet and British operations in the Pacific were unknown.

As the October plan was circulated through the various joint and combined planning agencies, almost everyone expressed dissatisfaction with it. The Combined Planners could not reach agreement on it and laid it aside for the time being. The Senior Team of the JWPC favored the first course of action over the second and recommended that Hokkaido be invaded in 1945 and Honshu the following spring. They did not agree that there were not good prospects of defeating Japan by October 1945, and they objected to the importance the plan attached to the assistance of the British Fleet in the Central Pacific. They insisted that any British forces sent to the Pacific should be well balanced and self-sustaining.

The Joint Staff Planners were less sure that invasion was necessary. Brigadier General Haywood S. Hansell still thought that the problems in conducting a B-29 offensive from China could be solved. Rear Admiral B. H. Bieri, too, thought that "when the full weight of our air and naval power is deployed against [Japan] we may find the road much easier than anticipated."[1]

The Joint Strategic Survey Committee criticized the plan as too conservative. They saw a number of reasons for greater optimism. In their opinion, isolation of Japan by a sea and air blockade, a continual whittling down of her fleet, and air bombardment of her most vulnerable cities and factories would eliminate the need for invasion, except possibly by an occupying force against little or no opposition. Thus, there was a good chance that Japan could be defeated much more cheaply and as quickly by invasion. Besides, with the tide running so strongly in Allied favor in Europe, there was a growing possibility that Germany would fall by the spring of 1944. Further, sufficient progress had been made toward an understanding with the USSR to warrant preparation of planning studies based on the Soviet's participation in the war against Japan. This last, no doubt, was said with the knowledge that Stalin had agreed at the Moscow Conference, held the month before, to enter the war against Japan after Germany was defeated. They therefore suggested that the plan again be revised, based on more favorable assumptions and on a more aggressive, imaginative, and

---

[1] Mins, JPS 109th mtg, 27 Oct 43, Item 1.

optimistic approach. These were comments one might not have expected from a group of supposedly conservative "elder statesmen."[1]

The Joint Chiefs discussed the plan while they were aboard ship en route to Cairo and the SEXTANT Conference on 15 November 1943.[2] Admiral King said he was astounded at the plan to invade Hokkaido instead of Formosa in 1945 as Hokkaido did not "loom up as important" in any of the currently planned campaigns. General Marshall seemed similarly concerned. He felt that a plan to approach Japan from the north ignored the vulnerability of Japan's oil sources to the south. Furthermore, it ignored the possibility of neutralizing such bases as Truk through carrier strikes, thus avoiding the need to seize them. In answer, Admiral Cooke pointed out that for the blockade and bombing to be most effective, it was not sufficient to cut off Japan's communications to the south; it was also necessary to reach targets in Manchuria. Admiral King then asked why Kyushu had not been chosen. It seemed to him to be more a logical objective of the current advances, and it also was in range of targets in Manchuria as well as other vital targets throughout Japan's defensive inner zone. Admiral Cooke replied that Kyushu had been considered but that the probable build-up of defenses there made the problems and risks of an invasion too great.

---

[1] Memo, Adm Willson for Adm King, 11 Nov 43, sub: Plans for Defeat of Japan, filed with min J.C.S. 123d mtg, 15 Nov 43. Adm Willson claimed to express his colleagues' views as well as his own.

[2] The Conference at Cairo carried the code name SEXTANT, while the interlude at Tehran with Stalin was called EUREKA.

Admiral King then read Admiral Willson's memorandum referred to above. In the end, the Joint Chiefs returned the plan to the Joint Planners for reconsideration in light of the comments of the JSSC and those of the Joint Chiefs themselves. Later at Cairo the Combined Chiefs also directed the combined planners to reconsider the plan. While the heads of State and the Combined Chiefs were away talking to the Soviets in Tehran, the planners worked on a revision of their plan.[1]

A New Plan at Cairo

The planners had to explore a number of new ideas if they hoped to get better acceptance of their revised plan. A week of intensive work ensued, involving discussions with the logistics experts and preparation of a number of preliminary papers. In the end, they seemed to re-embrace a strategy more in accord with their pre-October plan views. On 2 December the new plan was presented to the Combined Chiefs.[2] It was based on the following three assumptions:

    a. The possibility that invasion of the principal Japanese islands may not be necessary and the defeat of Japan may be accomplished by sea and air blockade and intensive air bombardment from progressively advanced bases. The plan, must, however, be capable of expansion to meet the contingency of invasion.

    b. The possibility that Germany may be defeated as early as the spring of 1944.

---

[1] At Tehran Stalin confirmed for the U.S. and British representatives Molotov's earlier assurances to U.S. Ambassador Harriman that the Soviets would enter the war against Japan after the defeat of Germany.

[2] C.P.S. 86/7, "Overall Plan for the Defeat of Japan," 30 Nov 43, is in ABC 381 Japan (8-27-42), Sec. 6.

c. The possibility that the USSR may enter the war against Japan early after the defeat of Germany.

Once again the long-range plan provided for an intermediate and not for a final objective. The objective was to obtain positions "from which we can conduct intensive air bombardment and establish a sea and air blockade against Japan, and from which to invade Japan proper if this should prove to be necessary."

This main effort against Japan was to be made in the Pacific and not from China or Southeast Asia. Within the Pacific the two main routes would remain those through the Mandated Islands from the Central Pacific and along the New Guinea-Netherlands East Indies-Philippine axis. They were to be mutually supporting, with transfers of naval and other resources between the two being effected as necessary. However, in case of conflict in timing and allocation of means, due weight would "be accorded to the fact that operations in the Central Pacific promise/d/ at /that/ time a more rapid advance toward Japan and her vital lines of communication; the earlier acquisition of strategic air bases closer to the Japanese homeland; and, of greatest importance, /were/ more likely to precipitate a decisive engagement with the Japanese Fleet." The aim would be a converging assault in the Formosa-Luzon-China area in the spring of 1945. Operations in other areas would be subsidiary, with the possibility that the North Pacific area would jump in importance if Russia entered the war.

Redeployment of forces from other theaters received considerable attention in the plan. This would have to begin at the earliest practicable date. The bulk of the U.S. naval forces was already in the Pacific, and virtually all the B-29's were scheduled for the Pacific and China Theaters. After Germany's defeat additional air forces would be shifted from Europe and within a few months about 40 U.S. divisions and supporting troops would be deployed in the Pacific.

Deployment of British forces in the Pacific had often been a subject of combined, joint, and theater discussions, but this was the first combined long-range plan in which it received detailed attention. Tentative conclusions of the planners were that British naval forces available by the spring of 1945 could be supported logistically and should operate from advance bases in the Bismarck and Solomons area in order to cover operations of the Southwest Pacific forces or to cooperate with the U.S. Fleet in the Central Pacific. The planners recognized that manpower limitations would prevent the manning of new bases by the British until after Germany's defeat.

It was estimated that the British would require nine months to reorganize, train, and transport each division redeployed to the Pacific. The target was to be four British divisions based on Australia. Australian and New Zealand forces would continue their Pacific operations, and deployment of Canadian forces would have to be discussed with the Canadian Government.

Finally, there was a summary of DRAKE, a plan for bombing Japan from the Kweilin-China area.

The JSSC found the new plan much more to their liking than the October plan. Their only significant criticism was its failure to establish the Central Pacific unequivocally as the main route of advance. In their words:

> The history of our discussions with the British concerning the strategic concept for Europe clearly demonstrates the continuous difficulties which arise when the primacy of the operations in one part of the theater is not clearly set forth and accepted -- but remains the subject of debate whenever operations are being considered in another part of the same theater. It is most desirable that we should profit by this experience and have no question in our own minds as to where the primary effort is to be made in the Pacific.[1]

The plan also met a favorable response from the members of the JCS when they returned to Cairo from Tehran. Both Admiral King and General Marshall were prepared to approve it from the first. But before reaching a decision, the JCS listened to Major General Richard K. Sutherland, General MacArthur's chief of staff, who argued against the view of the JSSC regarding the primary route of advance.[2] General MacArthur had insisted from the first that the Philippines were the keystone of the whole structure of Japanese conquests and holdings in the Pacific. First, their importance vis-a-vis the Marianas had to be argued, and later, their importance vis-a-vis Formosa and the China Coast. Actually, Sutherland did not argue against the China Coast as an objective but contended that the proper way to that objective was through the Philippines. Seizure of initial positions

---

[1] Memo, J.C.S. 614, "Plan for the Defeat of Japan," 2 Dec 43, in ABC 381 Japan (8-27-42), Sec. 6.

[2] Mins, Mtg, JCS 133d mtg, 3 Dec 43, Item 5.

in Mindanao would immediately cut off Japan from her vital supply of oil and would place Allied forces in the most favorable position possible for decisive attacks upon Japanese shipping. In addition, he contended, an attack on the Philippines would likely provoke a major fleet action.

Having established the Philippines as the major strategic objective short of Japan itself, General Sutherland went on to show why the best route to the Philippines was from the Southwest Pacific. In sum, probably his most cogent arguments amounted to two. First, in contrast to Central Pacific operations, advance along the axis into the heart of the enemy's southern empire would reduce Japan's war-making power beyond the mere attrition of her forces incident to the fighting during the advance. Second, it was the only route using the most effective combination of land, sea, and air power. While recognizing the great and growing effectiveness of carrier-based air power, only land-based air power, claimed General Sutherland, could maintain unrelenting pressure against the enemy. Continually applied from successive bases along the Southwest Pacific route of advance, land-based air power could, in combination with other forces, develop a momentum which the stop and start, largely independent operations projected in the Central Pacific could never achieve.

Sutherland did admit that diversionary operations in Southeast Asia and in the Central Pacific would be helpful. He presented a breakdown of Japanese forces which were deployed in an arc from Burma through the Netherlands East Indies, the Solomons, and the Japanese Mandates. They formed a defense perimeter of interlocking air and naval bases, supported by defense garrisons and mobile ground forces. Supporting operations against the western and eastern extremities could pin down large enemy forces, especially large ground forces in the west and large naval forces in the east.

To carry out his strategy General MacArthur had prepared a plan called RENO III, which scheduled the invasion of Mindanao on 1 February 1945. This schedule, General Sutherland pointed out, was based on the use of limited resources and in the knowledge "that the vitally necessary amphibious means would be largely devoted to an attack against the islands of the Central Pacific." Speed of execution would be in proportion to the means provided.

But the Joint Chiefs were no more persuaded by General Sutherland than they had been by the arguments of the JSSC. They were interested in speed, but they were not convinced that this could best be achieved by too exclusive a commitment to either route of advance or to objectives as distant as Mindanao and Palau (in the western Carolines).[1] Instead, they preferred, in the words of the plan, to "insure that the sequence of operations remain flexible and that preparations are made to take all manner of short cuts made possible by developments

---

[1] Specific operations for 1944 in support of the Long-Range Plan were approved separately at Cairo. MacArthur was to advance only so far as western New Guinea (the Vogelkop), and Nimitz was to take Ponape and Truk (in the eastern and central Carolines) and to go from there to the Marianas. See Morton, *Strategy and Command*, Chap. xxix, pp. 24 - 31.

in the situation."¹ Presumably their thinking agreed with a statement prepared by General Handy and read by General Marshall to the JCS:

> 1. This is a paper to which all our planners, as well as the British Planners, have agreed. The subject has been worked on on the Combined Planning level since last June. All viewpoints have been considered.
>
> 2. This paper in effect agrees to put the main effort of the war against Japan in the Pacific. It does not attempt to establish at this time any long range main effort within the Pacific Area. A great advantage of the plan is its flexibility in allowing the Joint Chiefs at any time to take advantage of the situation as it develops. By accepting this paper we leave all discussions of the Central and Southwest Pacific to the Joint Chiefs of Staff. In effect it gives the Joint Chiefs of Staff almost complete liberty of action in the Pacific without reference to the British Chiefs of Staff.²

After General Sutherland's recitation the JCS went into a closed session. With only some minor changes, they agreed to recommend approval of the plan to the Combined Chiefs of Staff.

Agreement at Last

When placed before them at Cairo, the British Chiefs were pleased with the plan, especially the statement that the main effort should be in the Pacific. It provided one more argument against expanded operations in Burma. They had been disturbed by the opinion of Admiral Mountbatten, the Supreme Allied Commander of SEAC, "that once the operations in North Burma were undertaken, either they would have to be continued to complete the capture of the whole of Burma or, alternatively, our forces would have to withdraw when the monsoon

---

¹ Quoted by Matloff, *Strategic Planning, 1943-1944*, p. 374.

² Memo, Maj Gen Handy, ACofS OPD, for Gen Marshall, 3 Dec 43, no sub, OPD Exec 5, Item 15, Folder 4; Cline, *Washington Command Post*, pp. 335 - 36.

stopped." Field Marshall Alan Brooke feared that Burma might become a huge vacuum, drawing forces away from the main effort. To keep this danger clearly in view, a fourth assumption was added to the plan, to wit: "The possibility that a full campaign in Burma may have to be carried out following on the TARZAN operation."[1] With that the Combined Chiefs approved the plan as amended, in principle, "as a basis for further investigation and preparation, subject to final approval by the Combined Chiefs of Staff."[2]

If this was short of unqualified approval, it represented the nearest thing yet to concensus of combined views. Here at last was an approved plan specific enough and yet broad enough to guide American strategic planners in Washington and in the theater of the Pacific until the end of the war. For over six months and through three successive high-level strategy conferences the development of the long-range plan for the defeat of Japan had been treated as a combined British-American problem. Thereafter it became once again an almost exclusively American problem. Only one decision on the highest plane of grand strategy remained to be made, and that was the decision to invade or not to invade Japan. If invasion should

---

[1] TARZAN was an operation of the Ledo forces (American and Chinese) against Myitkyina in North Burma. See Charles F. Romanus and Riley Sunderland, Stilwell's Command Problems (Washington: U.S. Government Printing Office, 1956), pp. 51 - 52. Supra, p.   , for the other assumptions.

[2] Approved on 6 Dec 43. John Ehrman, Grand Strategy, Vol. V; August 1943 - September 1944 (London: H.M. Stationery Office, 1956), p. 192.

come, it would be overwhelmingly an American operation. A second major decision yet to be made was who should command the final operations against Japan. The nature of this decision placed it on a lower level than the first but the two were intimately related. A third major decision yet to be made was a more specific selection of the great intermediate objective in that area described loosely in the plan as the "Formosa-Luzon-China area." It, too, was closely related to the second and first major decisions and was virtually the same as what might be called yet a fourth major decision -- the choice between the Southwest Pacific and Central Pacific axes of advance.

All these remaining deicsions could and, in the event, would be made within the framework of this plan. It had virtually all the advantages and none of the disadvantages of a plan which made those decisions at that early date. No further work on the long-range plan, as such, was undertaken for the rest of the war.

CHAPTER V

THE LAST TWO YEARS OF WAR: REACHING THE FINAL DECISIONS

The ink had scarcely dried on the agreements reached at Cairo when the commanders in the Pacific and the planners in Washington began to question some of their provisions. This applied not so much to the Long-Range Plan itself as to the specific operations approved for 1944 in support of the plan.[1] Some of the opposing views were aired at an inter-theater planning conference held at Pearl Harbor on 27 and 28 January 1944. Earlier in the month Nimitz had invited MacArthur and Halsey to send representatives to confer with his staff. The subject of their discussions was the cooperation of the two commands in the coming operations for the seizure or control of the Bismark Archipelago.[2] MacArthur's representatives were General Sutherland, General Kenney, and Rear Admiral Thomas C. Kinkaid -- his chief of staff, his air force commander, and his naval commander, respectively. The delegation from the South Pacific included Rear Admiral Robert B. Carney and Lieutenant General Millard F. Harmon, who were Admiral Halsey's chief of staff and army forces commander.

---

[1] A table listing all these operations is reproduced in Morton, *Strategy and Command*, Chap. xxix, p. 30.

[2] Agenda and transcript of the conference are inclosed in ltr from CINCPAC-CINCPOA to COMINCH, 29 Jan 44, sub: Conference Between . . . Pacific Ocean Areas, and . . . Southwest Pacific Area. A cy filed in OPD 334.8 Sec, Case 125.

The Theaters Agree

The conferees agreed almost unanimously that bases on the China coast would have to be seized; that the only way to China was via the Philippines; and that the best route to the Philippines was via New Guinea and not the Central Pacific. There was no enthusiasm for going into Truk; most thought it could be neutralized and by-passed. Neither was there much support for operations against the Marianas. General Kenney called the plan to base B-29's there a "stunt," and Rear Admiral Charles H. McMorris, representing Admiral Nimitz, had little faith in the effectiveness of the plan. Nimitz was skeptical of the ability of bombardment, even from bases in China and Korea, to force Japan to surrender.[1]

The Joint Chiefs Disagree

No such unanimity existed in Washington. On 8 February the Joint Chiefs met and discussed Pacific strategy, and on the same day Admiral King wrote to General Marshall criticising General MacArthur on a number of counts.[2] MacArthur, he claimed, instead of complying with a recent JCS directive to revise his RENO III plan, had sent General Sutherland to Washington to argue for a revision of the strategy agreed to at Cairo. Further, he could not agree to MacArthur's plan to use British naval task forces, the support of which would be a burden to the U.S. Navy. His most vehement objection was to

---

[1] Memo, Col Ritchie for Gen Handy, 4 Feb 44, sub: Brief on Pacific Conference . . . , Copy in ABC 384 Pacific (1-17-43) Sec 3-A.

[2] Memo, King for CofS, 8 Feb 44, sub: CinCSWPac Despatch C 121702, February 1944. Exec 2, Item 11.

MacArthur's plan to continue using the bulk of the South Pacific forces in operations in the Southwest Pacific.

General Marshall replied two days later in a memorandum worth quoting entirely. Its tone was one of unusual acerbity for him, but it is indicative of the atmosphere which often surrounded Army-Navy debate on Pacific strategy

> With reference to your memorandum of February 8th regarding the Pacific situation, I gathered the impression Tuesday /apparently referring to the JCS meeting of 8 February/ that many of the statements were made from the standpoint of an advocate or counsel and that the problem was not being approached with the view purely to its critical examination to determine the best course of action, leaving aside personalities, areas, command, service prestige, etc. It also was apparent, in my opinion, that we have a tremendous potential force in that region provided we conform to the basic principle of mass.
>
> There is a definite and almost purely Naval consideration as to what constitutes an undue hazard to our Naval power in the Pacific. However, this need only be related to the choice of successive objectives as there is no proposal by MacArthur to exercise command over the Pacific Fleet. He is concerned regarding the immediate task force that escorts and launches his amphibious enterprises.
>
> We have struggled since the outbreak of the war over questions of command in various regions of the Pacific from the Aleutians to Australia. The time has now come, in my opinion, to divorce from our minds any thought other than a purely objective purpose to secure the maximum result in the shortest time from the means available.
>
> The points raised by MacArthur, the record of the recent conference in Honolulu, the discussions Tuesday afternoon, recent events and developments in the Pacific, all taken together indicate to me the necessity for a re-examination of our Pacific strategy.

In your memorandum you state that MacArthur has not submitted a plan to carry out the Combined Chiefs of Staff decision, while Admiral Nimitz has done so. My understanding from the discussions to date is that both General MacArthur and Admiral Nimitz have been planning to use a considerable portion of the South Pacific forces, whose redisposition is now under consideration. Neither MacArthur's plan (RENO III) nor Nimitz' plan (GRANITE) carried out the decisions of the Combined Chiefs of Staff without asking for additional forces. Therefore the scale and timing of future operations are not clear-cut and cannot be until the Joint Chiefs of Staff inform the commanders concerned of the extent to which their requirements can be met. There appears to be a general agreement that the eventual defeat of Japan requires that we establish ourselves in force on the East Coast of China and there also appears to be a general acceptance that Luzon must be the stepping stone. There is no agreement, however, as to the way in which this shall be done. The present decision, which was largely for planning purposes only, of the Combined Chiefs of Staff, calls for an advance along two axes in the Pacific but does not carry through to the final establishment on the China coast. I therefore believe that a new directive is called for and my suggestion is that we issue instructions to the Strategic Survey Committee along the lines of the attached draft.

General Arnold concurs with me in the foregoing.

The point you raise about MacArthur's staff organization I will cover in a separate memorandum. [1]

War Department planners were not in full agreement with MacArthur's strategy, however. Brigadier General F. N. Roberts, the Army's Joint Planner (having succeeded General Wedemeyer), did not agree that Mindanao was a necessary stepping stone to Luzon or that it was otherwise a vital strategic objective. On the other hand, he considered the Marianas important for a number of reasons. [2]

---

[1] Exec 2, Item 1b.

[2] Memo, F. N. R. for Gen Handy, 8 Feb 44, no sub. OPD Exec 2, Item 11.

When the Joint Chiefs turned to the JSSC for their recommendations, those senior planners simply reaffirmed their earlier views. They favored Nimitz' plan GRANITE and recommended that Southwest Pacific operations support it.[1] General Marshall, at least, was still not ready to make such a clearcut decision in favor of one route. Nor were all the planners convinced that the main effort would be made in the Central Pacific. The Army's logistic planners argued strongly in favor of an advance along the New Guinea-Mindanao axis.[2]

Speed-up in the Pacific

On 29 February the strategists were suddenly presented with a new development. The Admiralty Islands on the north shore of the Bismark Sea were scheduled to be invaded by 45,000 men on 1 April. Although confronted with conflicting intelligence reports, General MacArthur, in one of the boldest tactical moves of the war, decided to make a 1,000 man reconnaissance in force into the area, 32 days ahead of D-Day. The move was a success; MacArthur ordered the force to stay and reinforced it quickly.[3] Then on 5 March he informed Marshall of his plan to leap several hundred miles in his next operation in New Guinea, going all the way to Hollandia. The New Guinea approach began to look better.

---

[1] Their report, J.C.S. 713, entitled "Strategy in the Pacific" and dated 16 Feb 44 is in ABC 384 Pacific (1-17-43), Sec. 3-A.

[2] Brief, 1 Mar 44, sub: Operations in the Pacific. OPD 381 Security, Case 301. This is a brief of a study made sometime earlier.

[3] For an account of this decision and its significance, see John Miller, Jr., "MacArthur and the Admiralties," an essay in Kent Roberts Greenfield, ed., Command Decisions (New York: Harcourt, Brace and Co., 1959), pp. 210 - 223.

At last on 12 March 1944 a new directive went out to the two senior commanders in the Pacific. Both Kavieng and Truk would be by-passed. MacArthur was to complete the occupation of the Admiralties, take Hollandia on 15 April, additional positions through the spring and summer, and Mindanao on 15 November. Nimitz was to seize the southern Marianas beginning 15 June and the Palaus on 15 September. The decision concerning Luzon and Formosa was deferred, but the Joint Chiefs assigned planning responsibility for the former to MacArthur, the latter to Nimitz. Target date for both was 15 February 1945.[1]

Luzon versus Formosa[2]

During the spring of 1944 the JWPC developed plans for seizing Formosa and outline plans for taking Mindanao and Luzon, the last operation to be either in support of or in lieu of Formosa. The JSSC again criticized the planners for being too conservative. Nimitz and MacArthur had pulled off one success after another, but, in retrospect, they might have economized on the force committed to these operations and converted the savings into greater speed. They recommended, and the JCS approved, that there be conducted a continuing search for shortcuts. There should be no commitment to inflexible plans or concepts. They did not miss the opportunity to point once again to the advantages of going directly to Formosa, if possible,

---

[1] Msg, JCS to CINCSWPA and COMGENCENTPAC, 12 Mar 44, CM-OUT 5137.

[2] For another account of the Luzon-Formosa debate, see Robert R. Smith, "Luzon versus Formosa" in <u>Command Decisions</u> pp. 358 - 373.

138

skipping the Philippines. They apparently did not think of an early approval of this plan as a commitment to an inflexible course of action.[1]

The Urge for Speed

This urge for greater speed fed on reverses as well as successes. Continued success in Europe promised an early shift to the Pacific of the means for a greater effort. Yet there were signs of war weariness that spring, even in America. If, by the time of Germany's collapse, the war against Japan had not make good progress, there might not remain enough spirit to push it to the final objective -- unconditional surrender.

In South China the Japanese offensives were threatening the complete collapse of Chinese resistance. A quick move to Formosa and the China Coast might save that situation; and if such a move could not be taken in time, then a principal reason for going there in the first place would be lost and Formosa itself might be by-passed. Moreover, intelligence reports showed that the Japanese were anticipating the next Allied operations and were moving greater strengths into Mindanao, Celebes, Halmahera, Vogelkop, and the Palaus. There was, then, all the more reason for by-passing these positions.[2]

---

[1] Their views are in a study, J.C.S. 713/6, entitled "Future Operations in the Pacific," 29 May 44. A copy in OPD 381 TS, Case 392.

[2] Msg, Marshall to MacArthur, Eyes Only, 24 Jun 44, CM-OUT 55718.

Under the compulsion of these ideas, Brigadier General William W. Bessell, Jr., and other Army members of the JWPC undertook a thorough study of the feasibility of an early invasion of Kyushu, southernmost of the Japanese home islands. They came to no clearcut conclusions but were skeptical of success. First, they doubted that command of air could be established and maintained without the support of land-based aircraft. In addition they doubted that it could be supported logistically, especially if the Japanese Navy did not, in the meantime, suffer a decisive defeat.[1]

On 13 June the Joint Chiefs asked MacArthur and Nimitz for their views of accelerating their schedules or of moving directly to Japan, by-passing Luzon and Formosa. The Pacific commanders encouraged neither of these ideas. Both insisted that it was necessary first to establish air and naval bases in the Central and Southern Philippines before moving on to Luzon or Formosa. Neither could see at that time any prospects for advancing their scheduled target dates. MacArthur was explicit and adamant in insisting that Luzon, too, was necessary before any further advance could be made. Nimitz was not sure; if a naval victory could be achieved or if enemy air on Luzon could be neutralized, he thought Luzon would not be necessary. MacArthur was equally sure that there could not be a long jump directly to Japan.

---

[1] 2d Draft, SS 265/3, 7 Jun 44, sub: Invasion of Kyushu after FORAGER /capture of Marianas/. ABC Kyushu (4 Jan 44). Sec. 1-13. Other planners were Cols T. D. Roberts and C. S. Babcock.

Nimitz failed to answer that question directly.[1]

The President Meets With His Commanders

Late in July, President Roosevelt, accompanied by Admiral Leahy, sailed for Hawaii for a personal meeting with Admiral Nimitz and General MacArthur. No new decisions were reached at the conference, but the two commanders explained to the Commander in Chief their views on future strategy (but not including their views on the ultimate strategy necessary for forcing Japan's unconditional surrender). The few first-hand and contemporary reports of the meetings are somewhat conflicting, but apparently both MacArthur and Nimitz reconfirmed their need and intent to go into the southern and central Philippines. MacArthur then expressed his conviction that Luzon had to be occupied. He based his arguments mainly on strategic considerations, but, as always, he pointed out the American political and moral obligation to liberate the loyal and long-suffering Filipinos. Nimitz then presented his plan for a movement direct to Formosa. The President was attentive but noncommittal.[2]

The Luzon versus Formosa struggle continued on through the summer and into the fall. In Washington Admiral King maintained a solid front with Admiral Cooke, Admiral Willson (Navy member of the JSSC),

---

[1] Msg, JCS to MacArthur and Nimitz, 13 Jun 44, CM-OUT 50007; msg, MacArthur to Marshall, 18 Jun 44, CM-IN 15058; msg, CINCPOA to COMINCH, 4 Jul 44, CM-IN 2926.

[2] Ltr, Marshall to Richardson, 20 Jul 44 and ltr, Richardson to Marshall, 1 Aug 44, copies of both in OCMH files (Bailey notes); memo, King for Marshall and Arnold, 9 Aug 44, no sub, in OPD 381 TS, Case 392/13. The last includes an extract from a letter from Nimitz.

and Rear Admiral B. H. Bieri (Navy member of the JPS) in favor of Nimitz' Plan GRANITE, i.e., Formosa first. The Army was not so well disciplined. Lieutenant General Joseph T. McNarney, an air officer and the Deputy Chief of Staff, consistently favored by-passing Luzon for Formosa. General Arnold's planners and the air force members of the joint committees had long supported the Formosa-China coast operations, but they began to waver and shift as Chiang Kai-shek's forces were pushed back farther from the coast. General Marshall, backed by his principal planning advisers, General Handy (Chief of OPD) and General Roberts (Army member of the JPS), was unwilling to make a decision until absolutely necessary. The situation was still fluid and liable to change; and while he recognized the theoretical advantages of the Formosa-China Coast area, he also saw great strategic value in Luzon and was impressed with the relatively low cost of seizing it. The firmest and most consistent opposition to the Formosa-China Coast operations came from Lieutenant General Brehon B. Somervell, Commanding General, Army Service Forces, and his logistics planners.

Virtually all of the commanders in the Pacific except Admiral Nimitz wanted to go to Luzon first, and there was a growing feeling that after Luzon, Formosa could be by-passed. MacArthur was not alone when he expressed his belief that Luzon, properly organized, could serve as the base for mounting an invasion of Japan, and that this could be done after seizing an island air base in the Ryukyus.[1]

---

[1] Msg, MacArthur to Marshall, 3 Aug 44, CM-IN 2479; Notes on Conference, August 7 at GHQ SWPA, 16 Aug 44, ABC 384 Pacific (1-17-43), Sec. 5.

Not only did MacArthur's subordinate commanders agree with him, so did General Richardson in Hawaii, and Admiral Halsey as well. On one occasion Admiral King asked Admiral Carney, Halsey's chief of staff, if he wanted "to make a London out of Manila." "No Sir," replied Carney, "I want to make an England out of Luzon."[1]

Leyte Ordered

General Marshall had been urging that a directive for immediate operations be given the Pacific commanders, and Admiral King finally agreed to this on 8 September. MacArthur was ordered to occupy Leyte with a target date of 20 December 1944, and Nimitz was directed to provide him with fleet support and assault shipping. The decision on Luzon and Formosa was again postponed, but MacArthur was told to plan for the first for 20 February and Nimitz for the latter for 1 March.[2] This decision proved to be the beginning of the end for the Formosa operation.

Events developed swiftly and dramatically in the next few days, reminiscent of the days six and one half months earlier in the Admiralties. Fast carrier task forces of Admiral Halsey's Third Fleet made a number of sweeps over the western Carolines and the southern and central Philippines on 7, 8, 12, and 14 September, meeting surprisingly little opposition and scoring great successes against Japanese shipping, aircraft, and shore installations. Halsey immediately recommended

---
[1] Quoted by Smith, "Luzon versus Formosa," in *Command Decisions*, p. 365.
[2] Msg, JCS to MacArthur and Nimitz, 9 Sep 44, CM-OUT 27648.

that the imminent operations against the Palaus, Yap, and Ulithi by Central Pacific forces be eliminated in favor of an immediate assault on Leyte. Admiral Nimitz readily agreed to eliminate Yap and to release to General MacArthur the III Amphibious Force, including the XXIV Army Corps, about to embark at Pearl Harbor for Yap. MacArthur knew from his intelligence reports that Japanese strength in the Central Philippines was far stronger than as reported by Halsey, yet he readily accepted Nimitz' offer. The Joint Chiefs were at that time in Quebec attending the OCTAGON Conference. Excusing themselves from dinner for a brief conference on the evening of 15 September, they accepted the recommendations of the Pacific commanders and directed MacArthur to invade Leyte on 20 October, thus stepping up the whole schedule of the Pacific War by 2 months. This was speed, flexibility, cooperation, and control at its best.[1]

Nimitz had up to this time loyally supported Admiral King's views, but it had long been clear that his personal convictions in favor of Formosa first were not strong. This was implicit in an act of his the very next day after receipt of the Leyte directive. On the 16th he asked his subordinate commanders for their views on by-passing Formosa and going to Okinawa in the Ryukyus and to Iwo Jima in the Bonins. General Richardson's response was entirely favorable. It may be assumed that other answers were similar, for this is exactly what

---

[1] There exist a number of brief accounts of this. See, e.g., Matloff, <u>Strategic Planning, 1943-1944</u>, pp. 512 - 13.

Nimitz recommended to King 12 days later.[1]

On the 21st MacArthur informed the JCS that he was now prepared to go to Luzon on 20 December, the date formerly scheduled for Leyte and 73 days prior to the target date for Formosa. After that, he suggested, Formosa would not be necessary. After "certain operations to the north" it should be possible to move directly to Kyushu.[2]

Luzon Ordered

Nimitz now withdrew his remaining support for the Formosa operations and proposed instead that he take Iwo Jima in late January and Okinawa beginning 1 March. King stood alone. Reluctantly, he agreed, and the Joint Chiefs ordered MacArthur to take Luzon on 20 December and for Nimitz to take one or more positions in the Bonins beginning 20 January and one or more positions in the Ryukyus beginning 1 March.[3]

Invasion Reconsidered

Although the 12 March 1944 directive had postponed the decision about operations in the great intermediate objective area (Luzon-Formosa-China Coast), no one at that time thought it could be put off until October. The Joint War Plans Committee therefore had several

---

[1] Ltr, Nimitz to Commander, Fifth Fleet, CG Tenth Army, Commanders Amphibious Forces, Pacific Fleet, Ser. 000113, 16 Sep 44, sub: CAUSEWAY Objective; Ltr, Richardson to CINCPOA, 27 Sep 44, same sub. Both ltrs incl in ltr Gen Richardson to CofS, sub: Strategy in the Pacific, 28 Sep 44. A cy in OPD 381 TS, Case 519.

[2] Msg, MacArthur to Marshall, 21 Sep 44, CM-IN 19803.

[3] Msg, JCS to MacArthur, Nimitz, and Stilwell, 3 Oct 44, CM-OUT 40782.

planning teams working simultaneously on future plans for the war against Japan. While separate plans for Formosa and Luzon were being prepared, one planning team was investigating the feasibility of by-passing that area and going straight to one of the home islands. Still another team, starting with the assumption that the intermediate objective area had been secured, attempted to outline the final operations against Japan. Late in the spring the members of this last team reported the result of their work in a long (11 pages including annexes) and thoughtful study.[1] They concluded early that the overall objective was inadequately stated in the Long-Range Plan approved at Cairo. At that time it had been expressed as follows:

> To obtain objectives from which we can conduct intensive air bombardment and establish a sea and air blockade against Japan, and from which to invade Japan proper if this should prove to be necessary.

Since that time the situation had changed. Advances had since been made in all theaters toward Japan. The Allies now had the benefit of greater experience and had available greater and growing human and material resources. "The statement of our present over-all objective," they said,

> does not take these changes into account. It reflects the fact that we were a long distance from Japan at that time and that our future operational plans were somewhat vague. It implies that it is quite possible to defeat Japan without an invasion. We consider this to be an overly optimistic attitude. While the bombing and blockade of Japan will have a considerable effect upon Japanese morale and their ability to continue the war, there is little reason to believe that such action alone is certain to result in the early unconditional surrender of Japan.

---

[1] J.P.S. 476, "Operations Against Japan, Subsequent to Formosa," 6 Jun 44. A copy in ABC 384 Pacific (1-17-43) Sec. 3-A. For more background on this study, see Cline, Washington Command Post, p. 337.

After elaborating on this statement they concluded that the concept of operations against Japan should include an invasion of the industrial heart of Japan. Acceptance of such a concept would insure proper planning for the necessary forces and for their logistical support; and that kind of planning would keep planners, the Joint Chiefs, commanders, and forces best prepared to take short-cuts as opportunities presented themselves. The over-all objective should therefore be restated to read as follows:

> To force the unconditional surrender of Japan by: (1) Lowering Japanese ability and will to resist by establishing sea and air blockades, conducting intensive air bombardment, and destroying Japanese air and naval strength.
>
> (2) Invading and seizing objectives in the industrial heart of Japan.

In the process of determining the conditions which should be brought about before invasion took place, the planners considered in some detail, first, the amount of destruction necessary to Japan's exterior and interior lines of communication, to her industrial plant, to her armed forces, and to her morale and, second, the kinds of bases necessary for conducting these operations. They rejected almost immediately the possibility of moving directly to Honshu or Shikoku and settled on China (a large area centering on Shanghai), Korea, Kyushu, or Hokkaido as possible "final objectives" and on areas along the China coast, in the Ryukyus, the Bonins and the Kuriles as possible "intermediate objectives."

The concluding recommendations were for operations which were remarkably similar to those actually carried out and to others which were ultimately approved. The planners recommended seizing objectives in the Bonins, in the Ryukyus, and on the China Coast (they assumed that Formosa was occupied), invasion of Kyushu on 1 October 1945 and finally the Tokyo Plain of Honshu on 31 December.

The Joint Staff Planners approved the plan and sent it to the JCS for their approval.[1] General Marshall and Admiral King had just returned from Europe, where they had stayed through the critical period following the cross-channel invasion of Normandy. They studied the plan early in July. Admiral King made one recommendation for an amendment, which the JCS accepted, and it was approved on 11 July.[2]

Admiral King's acceptance of the plan, with its new concept for winning the Pacific War, did not mean that he accepted the inevitability of invasion. He simply accepted it as a concept for guiding future plans. Since any major operation had to receive the prior approval of the JCS anyway, he would have ample opportunity in the months ahead to oppose or propose any strategy or operation as he saw fit.

---

[1] A copy of the plan, J.C.S. 924, "Operations Against Japan Subsequent to Formosa," 30 Jun 44, is in ABC 381 Japan (1-17-43) Sec. 4.

[2] Disposition Form, OPD of G-2, 14 Jul 44, sub: Operations Against Japan Subsequent to Formosa. OPD TS, Case 408/4.

On the same date that the JCS approved the plan, they recommended its approval to the CCS. The British never wavered in advocating a priority of effort for the war against Germany. They viewed this as the most vital concept of combined strategy and they protected it zealously, above all others. After the usual expression of concern and the usual reassurance by the JCS that the new statement would not compromise that concept, the plan was approved.[1] The new statement of the objective was reaffirmed by the CCS at the OCTAGON (second Quebec) Conference in September and included in the Final Report to the President and Prime Minister.[2]

Reorganizing the Pacific

The question of command was always near the surface and often plainly visible in the dispute over Pacific strategy. Everyone admitted the theoretical advantages of unity of command. In fact, at one time or another, almost everyone concerned put forth a strong recommendation for it. But since the decision of March 1942 to divide the Pacific Theater between SWPA and POA the question had been manageable if greatly troublesome. But now that forces from both major commands were being funneled into the Philippine operations, the need for a new arrangement for the future became more pressing.

---

[1] The final reply from the British Chiefs, dated 29 Jul 44, and the final reply of the JCS, dated 4 Aug 44, are in ABC Japan (8-27-42), Sec. 6.

[2] Cline, *Washington Command Post*, p. 339.

At least as early as the summer of 1944 General MacArthur expressed his views that the time was fast approaching when the division of command by area would be no longer logical or efficient. He recommended the creation of one army command and one navy command with the former being responsible for major land campaigns and the latter for operations at sea. When the Philippines operations began, the sea lanes would have been cleared, declared MacArthur, and thereafter operations would be primarily against large land masses. After Manila was secure he and Nimitz should set up side by side there and begin making their plans for invading Japan. In conversation with Major General John E. Hull, Chief of Theater Group, OPD, he stated that Admiral Nimitz had agreed with his views on numerous occasions but that he invariably reversed himself after talking to Admiral King.[1]

MacArthur's view was generally the one which the War Department planners defended during the next several months of negotiations with the Navy. At times, however, there was a not too enthusiastic proposal by army planners for a true joint (MacArthur-Nimitz) command. Although the idea was presented to MacArthur, who rejected it, it seems never to have been seriously proposed to the Joint Chiefs.[2]

---

[1] Ritchie notes for Discussion with Gen Marshall /16 Aug 44/, ABC 384 Pacific (1-17-43), Sec. 5; msg, MacArthur to Marshall, 17 Dec 44, CM-IN 16870.

[2] See, e.g., Draft Memo from CofS, for JCS, Tab B to memo, Col Lincoln for Gen Hull, 22 Dec 44, sub: Command Relationship in the Pacific. ABC 323.31 POA (1-29-42), Sec. 3-A.

The Navy was not the least inclined to believe that their work was over after the Philippines land campaign began. The invasion of Japan would commit virtually the entire Pacific Fleet to its support. But prior to this the Navy anticipated some important, perhaps decisive operations along the China Coast and within the seas of the Western Pacific. Nimitz suggested simply an amendment to the area commands. He proposed that one theater of the Pacific Ocean Areas, exclusive of Japan, be created; that he be made responsible for the amphibious phase of the invasion; and that thereafter Japan be designated a separate theater under the JCS. The navy planners approved the plan, and it was essentially this plan which Admiral King proposed to the JCS on 8 March 1945.[1]

The final agreement was close to the Army's proposal.[2] On 3 April MacArthur, in addition to his command of SWPA, was designated Commander in Chief, U.S. Army Forces, Pacific, with control of all army forces in the Pacific except in the North and Southeast areas and except for the Twentieth Air Force.[3] His position was now much like that of Nimitz, who remained Commander in Chief of the Pacific Fleet and of the Pacific Ocean Areas. The JCS would issue operational directives, assign missions,

---

[1] Ltr, Nimitz to King, 24 Jan 45, sub: Future Operations, Ser 000134, extracts in OCMH files (Bailey Notes, Sec. IV); memo, Adm King for Adm Leahy, Gen Marshall, Gen Giles, 8 Mar 44, sub: Directive for the Reorganization and Future Operations in the PACIFIC THEATER, OPD 384 TS, Case 1/29.

[2] According to Gen Marshall in a memo to Gen Hull, 3 Apr 45, sub: Pacific OPD 381 TS, Case 99/6. Adm Leahy OK'd the agreement and wired the general sense of it to the President in Warm Springs. The President approved it in what must have been his last military decision.

[3] This Air Force of VLR B-29's had been abuilding and in operation for some time. It was commanded by General Arnold through his deputy, General Harmon. Units were located in the CBI, SWPA, and POA.

and fix command responsibilities for major campaigns. Primarily to assure Nimitz' continued responsibility for the Ryukyus operations, forces currently under command of each area commander would not be transferred except by mutual agreement or by JCS directive.[1]

An operational directive was approved on the same date. Nimitz would complete his operations in the Ryukyus in accordance with his former directive; continue operations to secure the sea communications to and within the Western Pacific; cooperate with CINCAFPAC in his operations; and continue with plans for operations against the coast of China. Preparations for this last was to be limited to the "assembly of necessary special equipment . . . in a priority which /would/ not jeopardize timely preparations for the invasion of Japan." MacArthur was to continue operations in the Philippines, support the Ryukyus operations, plan for other subsidiary operations, and plan and prepare for the invasion of Japan, cooperating with CINCPAC.[2]

General Arnold was not satisfied with the organization and mission of the Twentieth Air Force. He soon recommended the creation of a U.S. Army Strategic Air Force (USASTAF) in the Pacific under the command of General Carl Spaatz, who was still commanding the strategic bomber forces in Europe. The main opposition to his views came from Admiral King and, to a lesser extent, from General MacArthur. Nevertheless,

---

[1] Msg, JCS to MacArthur, Nimitz, and Arnold, 3 Apr 45, CM-OUT 62773.

[2] Msg, JCS to MacArthur, Nimitz, and Arnold, 3 Apr 45, CM-OUT 62774.

he succeeded on 10 July, thus completing the rearrangement of the command structure in the Pacific until MacArthur was appointed Supreme Commander for the Allied Powers on 15 August.[1]

OLYMPIC – Final Negotiations

When the 3 April directives were issued, the campaign in the Ryukyus had already begun. In fact the first landing had been made on Okinawa on 1 April, to begin the main operation of that campaign. Time was already pressing on the Joint Chiefs to issue a directive for the next major campaign. Immediately, they were to find that their command directive was imperfect and that they were far from done with the problem of command. For a while at least it was inextricably tied to the problem of whether to go next to Japan or to undertake additional preliminary operations either on the Asiatic mainland or in one or more of the island groups lying closer to Japan. Admiral King and his planners in Washington were the principal supporters of plans for additional operations. This support was inspired by a number of ideas. Among them were a desire to keep up the pressure against Japan during the period between Okinawa and Kyushu; the need for more air bases to support the invasion; the support which such operations, especially in the Kuriles, would give the expected Russian effort; and the constant hope by all and the positive belief by some that Japan could be forced to surrender by means short of invasion.

The members of the Joint War Plans Committee were among those who felt most strongly that it was wishful thinking to expect

---

[1] SWPA History, p. 441.

unconditional surrender without invasion. They were pessimistic that even invasion would force the Japanese to agree to unconditional surrender. The very idea, they pointed out, was foreign to the nature and experience of the Japanese. Throughout the war there had not been one instance of the surrender of an organized unit of the Japanese armed forces, even in the most hopeless situations. They estimated that thirty-six divisions would be required to carry out the invasion of Kyushu (Operation OLYMPIC) and Honshu (Operation CORONET) and that it could begin before the end of the year. A strategy of blockade and bombardment, on the other hand, would still require twenty-eight divisions, and the estimated time required for this strategy varied from several months to several years. There was no assurance that the latter would be cheaper, either, for it would require more of the expensive amphibious operations of the kind used in moving across the Pacific.[1] Experience in Europe and in the larger land masses of the Pacific, such as Leyte, Luzon, and Okinawa were leading to somewhat more hopeful estimates of the casualty rates of fighting in the home islands of Japan.

Admiral King, on the other hand, pointed to the many differences in the nature of the geography and of the enemy in the Pacific. He disagreed with the very idea of trying to compare the fighting in Europe with that in the Pacific. Moreover, he pointed to the great

---

[1] Msg, Marshall to MacArthur, Eyes Only, 12 Apr 45, CM-OUT 67098 for the expression of such an idea.

advantages which the Japanese Army would have in the fight in their homeland. There they would have room to maneuver and would not be so vulnerable to the overpowering air and naval power which the Allies had been able to bring to bear against them on small and isolated islands. At home they would also be near their bases of supply and reinforcement. Despite these feelings, King continued to approve of the need for planning for the invasion.

General MacArthur saw three possible courses of action open after the spring of 1945. The first was to continue to move westward to the coast of China and from there to deploy the maximum ampunt of air power against Japan in preparation for invasion. The second was also to continue westward to the mainland with a view to isolating Japan and then bombing her into submission. The third course was to capture Kyushu and install there the necessary air forces to cover the landing and fighting on Honshu. After analyzing each course of action, he concluded that the first, while certain of success, was the most expensive; that the second, while the least expensive, was not certain of succeeding and in any case would take an excessively long time, and that the third would achieve victory the quickest and at acceptable cost.[1]

Admiral Nimitz agreed that Kyushu should be invaded at the earliest date at which success could be assured. Until that date,

---

[1] Msg, MacArthur to Marshall, Eyes Only, 20 Apr 45, CM-IN 19089.

operations to isolate Japan should be continued. As a minimum he proposed securing Kikai Jima after Okinawa. He established a number of prerequisites for an early seizure of Kyushu. They included control of the sea and of the air and availability of the combat troops, of shipping, of supplies, and of a logistical organization to support the operation. All this should be ready for a target date no later than 1 November, as the heavy winter surfs beginning shortly after that date would make over-the-beach supply exceedingly difficult. If the conditions could not be met for an invasion during 1945, he recommended "occupation of the Chusan Archipelago followed by operations to control the Korea Strait."[1]

With Admiral Nimitz joining MacArthur in recommending an invasion of Kyushu, Admiral King immediately proposed that the Joint Chiefs of Staff issue a directive for the operation with a target date of 1 November. He was convinced that enough time remained to assemble the necessary resources provided the directive were issued quickly and the operation were given top priority. The Joint Chiefs could still cancel the operation as late as August or September if they should later decide against the operation.[2]

This was easier approved than accomplished. Nearly a month was to pass before the directive recommended by King went out to the

---

[1] Msg, Nimitz to King, MacArthur, Halsey, Spruance, and Kinkaid only, 28 Apr 45, CM-IN 26766.

[2] His proposal was circulated in J.C.S. 1331, "Proposed Issue of "OLYMPIC" Directive," 30 Apr 45. A copy is in ABC 384 Kyushu (4 Jul 44) Sec. 1-B.

commanders in the Pacific. The delay did not result from any lack of effort. Into the effort went personal conferences of all kinds, committee meetings, long memoranda, and radio messages among Marshall, King, MacArthur, Nimitz, joint planners, service planners, and theater planners. Negotiations were both long and tedious. The whole problem revolved about the question of division of responsibility between the two service commanders in the Pacific in the final operations against Japan. It was not the first time that the Joint Chiefs and their planners in Washington had wrestled with the problem of command in the Pacific Theater, but in the past they had been able to avoid the kind of details which it was necessary for them to meet this time. In the past such details had been/decided within each theater by the commander, but the command directive of 3 April provided that the JCS would fix such responsibilities in the future.

For the first week negotiations were conducted primarily between General Lincoln and Admiral Duncan. On 2 May Lincoln presented a draft directive for Duncan's consideration. The two critical paragraphs were the following:

    3. CINCAFPAC is responsible for the campaign in Japan of which OLYMPIC is the initial operation.

    4. CINCPAC is responsible for the plans and preparations for the amphibious and naval phases of the campaign in Japan and will cooperate with and assist CINCAFPAC in the execution of OLYMPIC.

By the 6th of May, after more discussion, this section had become:

b. CINCAFPAC-CINCSWPA:

(1) Is charged with the responsibility for the conduct of the campaign in KYUSHU.

(2) Will make plans and preparations for the continuance of the campaign in JAPAN and cooperate with CINCPAC in the plans and preparations for the naval and amphibious phases thereof.

c. CINCPAC-CINCPOA:

(1) Is charged with the responsibility of the conduct of the naval and amphibious phases of the OLYMPIC operation, in conformity with CINCAFPAC-CINCSWPA's plans for the campaign on land.

(2) Will cooperate with and assist CINCAFPAC in his plans and preparations for the campaign in JAPAN.

This still was not satisfactory to the Navy, and on 8 May General Lincoln reported to General Marshall the nature of the Army and Navy differences.

2. The Navy's argument is that to require Nimitz to make an amphibious plan "in conformity with" MacArthur's campaign plan subordinates Nimitz to MacArthur and also places Nimitz in the position where MacArthur could make him undertake an amphibious operation, which is militarily unsound. The Army stand is that once committed to going ashore in Japan, the battle in Japan is primary. All other phases of the operation must be built back from the air-ground battle and must be adjusted and conform to that battle. The Army recognizes that standard practice dictates that the naval commander can always refuse to go ashore in a particular area and in accordance with a particular plan if the Navy considers the amphibious operation infeasible. Hence, Admiral Nimitz is adequately protected.

3. Related to this point of difference is the question as to just where "primary responsibility" passes from Nimitz to MacArthur following the ICEBERG /Ryukyus/ campaign. In paragraph 4 of JCS 1259/5, the Joint Chiefs of Staff indicated they would invest a specific commander in chief of a service with primary responsibility for each operation or campaign. The Army planners' thought is that once ICEBERG is completed, the emphasis goes on the campaign against Japan proper and primary responsibility passes to MacArthur for the Japan campaign, including the primary responsibility for preparatory operations, which are principally

air operations. The Navy thought originally was that MacArthur's major interest started somewhere beyond the beaches of Kyushu at the conclusion of the naval and amphibious phases of OLYMPIC. The Army Planners consider that it is all one operation from the air preparation through the amphibious landing and on into the destruction of the enemy's forces in the major land battle. The Navy Planners now agree to some extent to this thought, but we have been unable to get it down in writing and consider that the matter should be left unwritten for the time being.

4. The Army concept and interpretation of the present setup in the Pacific, which makes the commander in chief of a service primarily responsible for specific operations and campaigns, indicated that the terms "CINCSWPA" and "CINCPOA" should be stricken out. But this is a minor point.

5. The Navy Planner wished to use the code word "OLYMPIC" and also, in the same paper, speak of the "invasion of Kyushu and campaign in Kyushu." This is a violation of security but was accepted as a minor point. To the Army Planners it was preferable to stick to the single term "OLYMPIC." There may be a hidden purpose in the wording but this is doubted. [1]

The two theater commanders concerned had little more success in their attempts to reach agreements under the terms of the 3 April directive. Their planning staffs met first in Guam in mid-April and the next month in Manila. After the first meeting of the Guam Conference, Admiral Nimitz reported to Admiral King that General Sutherland, General MacArthur's chief of staff,

advanced the view that all our previous command arrangements had been "unsatisfactory" and that unity of command was an unworkable "shibboleth." He further stated that in the future (post-ICEBERG) no Army troops would be allowed to serve under an admiral. . . . However, the essential garrisons of all positions in the Pacific Ocean Areas must remain under my operational control as long as I am responsible for those areas. . . . It appears that MacArthur expects to take over the Ryukyus and Kenny expects to take over air operations in the Ryukyus. [2]

---

[1] Memo, G. A. L. /Lincoln/ for CofS, 8 May 45, sub: Directive for Operations Against Japan. This and other papers relating to this period of Army-Navy negotiations are in ABC 323.31 POA (1-29-42), Sec. 3-A.

[2] Msg, CINCPAC to COMINCH, 14 Apr 45, inclosed in Memo, King for Marshall, 14 Apr 45, sub: Admiral Nimitz' Conference with General Sutherland. OPD 384 TS, Case 1/42.

Secretary Forrestal recorded some comments on the conference in his diary. They are interesting, if incomplete and possibly misleading:

> In mid-April there was a formal conference at Guam, almost on the level of international diplomacy, between delegates from the Southwest Pacific Area (MacArthur) and representatives of the Pacific Ocean Areas (Nimitz), in which MacArthur's people sought to secure command over all land and air forces in the Pacific, relegating to the Navy the minor role of purely naval support. "Since these ideas," Nimitz tartly reported to King "were consuming valuable time and delaying constructive planning," he finally authorized his representative to lay down the law on what the admiral would and would not surrender to the general. The Southwest Pacific delegation appears to have retired in discomfiture; "very little useful discussion," Nimitz reported, "has taken place concerning invasion plans and preparations, and the SWPA party was apparently not prepared for such discussion." [1]

MacArthur considered that his responsibilities for the invasion began long before the beachhead would be established. The most important pre-invasion operation was the air bombardment of the target area and of communications leading into the target area. This operation he expected to control; and the main base for these operations would be Okinawa. Nimitz, however, looked upon the Ryukyus as an important locality in the area for which he was responsible. In an important sense the disagreement was a manifestation of the different way in which the Army and Navy looked upon almost any position once it was captured and secured. To the Navy Okinawa was an important post guarding the line of communication on the way to China (or to areas to the north); while to the Army it was but another important stepping stone on the way to Japan. Just a difference in emphasis perhaps, but it was an important difference. But the most important conflict

---

[1] The Forrestal Diaries, ed. Walter Millis (New York: The Viking Press, 1951), pp. 45 - 46.

with MacArthur's position was Nimitz' view that all early phases of OLYMPIC, to include the seizure and firm control of a beachhead, was primarily his.

Later at the Manila conference considerable headway was made toward reaching a compromise. MacArthur gave a full report of the agreements reached in a message to Marshall. The all-important matter of control during the amphibious phase he reported as follows:

> (1) During the amphibious phase of an operation while control is exercised by CINCPAC, land-based air elements operating in the objective area will be controlled by CINCPAC, through a Commander designated by him. . . .
>
> (2) Similarly, after land-based air forces are established in an objective area and responsibility for air operations passes to CINCAFPAC, control of carrier-based air elements operating in an objective area will be exercised by the Commanding General, Far East Air Forces. . . .
>
> (3) Definition of objective areas, duration of amphibious phases and amount of land-based air available for operation in objective areas, will be established in the plans for specific operations.
>
> 3. Control of landing forces ashore, OLYMPIC operation.
>
> (A) The Commander, Fifth Fleet, will control the amphibious movement and landing through Commander, Amphibious Forces Pacific Fleet, who will in turn control the attack force of Group Commanders who are responsible for the amphibious operation at their respective objectives.
>
> (B) Control of forces ashore will pass to the Commander of each assault division or each separate landing force, after his arrival and establishment ashore, and upon his notification to the Commander of the corresponding naval attack group that he is ready to assume command of his forces ashore. The Commander of each assault division and separate landing force and the Commander of each naval attack group will promptly report to his next senior ground or naval Commander the time he assumes or relinquishes control of forces ashore.

(C) Control of forces ashore will pass to each Corps Commander within his respective area of operation after his arrival and establishment ashore and upon notification to the Commander of the corresponding naval attack force that he is ready to assume control of his forces ashore. Each Corps Commander will promptly report to the Commanding General, Sixth United States Army and the Commander, Amphibious Forces Pacific Fleet, respectively:

(1) The time each division and separate landing force and its corresponding naval attack group Commander assumes or relinquishes control of forces ashore.

(2) The time he himself assumes or relinquishes control of forces ashore.

(D) Division, separate landing force, and Corps Commanders who have assumed control of their forces ashore continue under control of the next senior naval attack force or Group Commander until their next Senior Army Commander assumes control of forces ashore.

(E) Control of forces ashore will pass to the Commanding General, Sixth United States Army, upon his announcement to the Commander, Amphibious Forces, Pacific Fleet, that he is ready to assume command of the forces ashore. The Commanding General, Sixth United States Army and the Commander Amphibious Forces Pacific Fleet, will promptly report to CINCAFPAC, CINCPAC and the Commander, Fifth Fleet, the time of assumption of control of forces ashore by the Commanding General, Sixth United States Army.

(F) Nothing in this type procedure limits the two Commanders in Chief from exercising under their general responsibilities such controls as extraordinary or unforeseen circumstances may necessitate.

* * * * * * * *

10. Foregoing agreements do not represent entirely the views of this headquarters. This is particularly true with regards to methods of control and coordination at Okinawa. They do represent, however, a solution in which it was possible to secure the concurrence of CINCPAC.[1]

---

[1] Msg, MacArthur to CofS (Info CG USAFPOA), 19 May 45, CM-IN 18105.

A first reading of this agreement might lead to the belief that MacArthur had acceded to the Navy's views. A few days later, however, after being asked by Marshall if he did not believe that he should control the amphibious assault through the appropriate naval commander, MacArthur replied with an emphatic concurrence and implied that that had been his intent all along. His understanding was, he said, that he was responsible for the campaign in Japan and that Nimitz was responsible for the amphibious phase of the invasion. The amphibious phase, in his view, consisted of mine sweeping, removing underwater obstacles, "et cetera," and the transport of the troops from ship to shore. Whereas Admiral Nimitz had expressed his view that OLYMPIC comprised two parts -- the naval and amphibious phase followed by the land campaign -- MacArthur thought greater emphasis should be put on its unity and continuity. Nimitz expected to maintain unity of command under himself until the Sixth Army Commander was established ashore with his headquarters and all its signal communications, two to four days after the assault. But the campaign would begin, according to MacArthur, with air preparation, long before the amphibious phase would begin; and since the air preparation would have such a profound effect on the outcome of the fight inland, it should be his responsibility.[1]

What really could not be separated, countered Admiral King, were the total naval responsibilities in the Pacific. These included not

---

[1] Msg, MacArthur to Marshall, Eyes Only, 21 May 45, CM-IN 20013.

only the current task of seizing and developing positions in the Ryukyus, but also operations to maintain and expand the control of sea communications to and within the Western Pacific and operations against the main islands of Japan, including the support of the land operations there, as well as the naval and amphibious phases of the invasion. Virtually all of the Pacific Fleet and, thus, the bulk of the U.S. Navy afloat would be committed to these various operations; and all those forces should be coordinated and commanded only by a headquarters such as existed at Guam under Admiral Nimitz.[1]

On 22 May there still remained two central points on which General Marshall and Admiral King were in complete disagreement, namely, Marshall's proposal that CINCAFPAC should control the amphibious assault through a naval commander and his belief that one commander should be designated as having primary responsibility for the campaign in Kyushu. He proposed a meeting of the JCS to settle them at once. King replied that there might be a simple misunderstanding in semantics which could be cleared up by a prior consultation of Admiral Cooke and General Hull. He readily admitted, he said, that CINCAFPAC had primary, even absolute, responsibility for the campaign in Kyushu. And it might be that he simply did not understand what Marshall meant by the "control of the amphibious assault."[2]

---

[1] Memo, King to Marshall, 19 May 45, sub: Operation OLYMPIC. OPD 381 TS, Case 135/14.

[2] Memo, Marshall to King, 22 May 45, sub: Operation OLYMPIC and memo, King to Marshall, 23 May 45, same sub. Both in OPD 381 TS, Case 135/14.

The conversations between Hull and Cooke proved that the differences were not merely semantic. The problem was squarely up to the Joint Chiefs themselves. They met in closed session on 25 May and agreed on the following directive which was sent to MacArthur, Nimitz, and Arnold that day:

    1. Pursuant to and in furtherance of directives contained in WAR 62773 and WAR 62774 both dated 3 April 1945, the following directive is issued and is effective on receipt.

        a. The Joint Chiefs of Staff direct the invasion of Kyushu (Operation OLYMPIC), target date 1 November 1945, in order to:

            (1) Intensify the blockade and aerial bombardment of Japan.

            (2) Contain and destroy major enemy forces.

            (3) Support further advances for the purpose of establishing the conditions favorable to the decisive invasion of the industrial heart of Japan.

        b. CINCAFPAC-CINCSWPA:

            (1) Is charged with the primary responsibility for the conduct of operation OLYMPIC including control, in case of exigencies, of the actual amphibious assault through the appropriate naval commander.

            (2) Will make plans and preparations for the continuance of the campaign in Japan and cooperate with CINCPAC in the plans and preparations for the naval and amphibious phases thereof.

        c. CINCPAC-CINCPOA:

            (1) Is charged with the responsibility for the conduct of the naval and amphibious (subject to para 1b (1) above) phases of the OLYMPIC operation, and will correlate his plans with CINCAFPAC-CINCSWPA.

            (2) Will cooperate with and assist CINCAFPAC in his plans and preparations for, and the conduct of, the campaign in Japan.

d. CG 20th Air Force, will cooperate in the plans, preparations, and execution of operation OLYMPIC and in the continuance of the campaign in Japan. At appropriate time, to be determined by the Joint Chiefs of Staff, the 20th Air Force will come under the direction of the appropriate command for support of operations directed above.[1]

Thus, the decision to invade, long considered inevitable by many officers, officially approved as an objective by the JCS on 11 July 1944, and confirmed by the CCS and heads of state at the second Quebec conference, was finally directed to be carried out. But this still was not the last time for the decision to be questioned and reaffirmed. The least convinced member of the JCS was Admiral Leahy, and he and many planners, especially in the Navy, questioned the idea in more or less subtle ways in the coming weeks. The President raised the question on at least two occasions -- once in June and again in July -- and after receiving the views of his civilian and military advisers reconfirmed the decision. The first occasion came on 18 June when the President called to the White House the JCS, the two service secretaries, and John J. McCloy, Assistant Secretary of War. At the meeting General Marshall read a digest of a much longer memorandum prepared for the President by the JCS. Before the meeting Mr. Truman had already announced that his decision would be based largely on economy of American lives and that the cost in terms of money and time would be relatively unimportant. General Marshall reviewed briefly the effects of Allied operations to date and the expected results of planned operations in the coming few months against the armed forces, the industry, the commerce, and the morale of the Japanese. While the

---

[1] Msg, JCS to MacArthur, Nimitz, and Arnold, 25 May 45, CM-OUT 87938.

Japanese air and naval forces were expected to be reduced to impotence by the fall, their Army would still be a strong fighting force. Even with continued blockade and bombing, ground defenses would continue to be strengthened in many respects the longer invasion were delayed. Estimates of whether and when the Japanese would agree to surrender without invasion were not optimistic. Marshall and his colleagues were not willing to estimate the casualties to be expected from an invasion of Kyushu, but they presented many reasons for their belief that they would be acceptable. "It is a grim fact," said Marshall,

> that there is not an easy, bloodless way to victory in war, and it is the thankless task of the leaders to maintain their firm outward front which holds the resolution of their subordinates. Any irresolution in the leaders amy result in costly weakening and indecision in the subordinates. . . .

Operations into Korea or China to encircle Japan further would likely be even more costly in lives as well as in time. The other members of the JCS and the service secretaries individually expressed their agreement, although Mr. Stimson still expressed his hopes "for some fruitful accomplishment through other means."[1] The President thereupon gave his consent. Together with Prime Minister Churchill he reconfirmed the decision at Potsdam on 24 July 1945, eight days after the first successful explosion of an atomic device at Alamogordo, New Mexico.[2]

---

[1] For an account of the 18 June meeting see "The Entry of the Soviet Union into the War Against Japan: Military Plans, 1941-1945," a Department of Defense document released 19 October 1955, pp. 76 - 85. It is a 107 page document prepared in response to inquiries by Members of the Congress and the press.

[2] Ibid., p. 90.

The decision to use the personal bomb was the personal one of the President, and all the deliberations preceding that decision were held at the highest level of the government. The military planners (there were only a very limited few who knew anything about it) had to perform their labors in complete disregard of the development of the atomic bomb and its potential value as a military weapon.[1] Its use therefore, and its great influence in hastening the end of the war came as an anticlimax to the performance of conventional strategic planning -- inapt as that description of an event so violent and so important in world history may seem. Wartime strategic planning was over; the military objectives had been achieved.

---

[1] Louis Morton, "The Decision to Use the Atomic Bomb," in Command Decisions, pp. 388 - 410.

SUMMATION: A REFLECTION AND APPRAISAL

Pre-War Planning and Preparation

The Japanese attack on Pearl Harbor, despite its jarring suddenness, was but the culmination of a long and gradually deepening involvement in the affairs of other nations and in the conflicts already raging in Europe and Asia. The status of the United States as a world power with far-flung interests had long been recognized by her citizens and was, in fact, a source of great pride to them. But even after the experience of World War I there persisted a reluctance to face squarely the possibility that military force, the ultimate sanction in international relations, might have to be invoked to protect those interests, that the invocation of lesser coersive measures or the ignoring or denying of threats to those interests might not be enough to avoid war.

The national policy for employing its coersive powers (including economic, diplomatic, and other non-violent pressures as well as the threat of military force) was designed first of all to deter any other nation from interfering with the political and economic interests of the United States. This policy was more sound than were the complementary plans for employing force once the deterrence failed. There were a number of reasons for this. For one thing the military planners simply underestimated the military force which would be necessary.

Especially underestimated were the army forces required, logistic as well as combat, both ground and air. Beyond this, and partly a cause of it, was the failure of other branches of the government to provide anywhere near the amount of military force which the military leadership did ask for.

As a result, the prelude to Pearl Harbor included three themes -- national policy, military plans, and military means -- which were poorly orchestrated; and the three began to harmonize only moments before the dramatic lifting of the curtain on Act I. This is not to say that they were composed independently, but too often it did seem so.

The most important interests of the United States outside the Western Hemisphere were in the area of the North Atlantic and its periperhal seas. Moreover, that flank was the most vulnerable, geographically and politically, to aggression. This had been clearly recognized by the military planners since at least as far back as the RED-ORANGE Plan. Yet, for a long time, Axis aggression in Europe presented a remote and indirect threat to American interests. Forward of U.S. defenses in the Atlantic stood the British Fleet and the French Army. But after the fall of France the threat was suddenly neither remote nor indirect. Mahan had seen clearly over half a century before that it was not the power of the U.S. Navy alone which had deterred all violations of the Monroe Doctrine. It was never more clear than in 1940. In keeping the aggressors at arms length U.S. policy provided for direct opposition to the Axis Powers as well as assistance to the enemies of the Axis. Massive assistance in lend-lease goods soon began to flow to Britain and, after June 1941, to Russia, much of it beginning in November, transported in armed U.S. merchantmen and escorted by the U.S. Navy. In countless other ways, also, the United States supported the victims of German and Italian aggression in a very unneutral fashion.

In a somewhat similar fashion China was aided in her struggle against Japan. Assistance to her began with loans but by December 1941 had been extended to more direct and more substantial aid. Lend lease to that beleaguered country began in May 1941, and in August Brigadier General John A. Magruder was sent there at the head of a mission to assist in receiving and maintaining Lend Lease materials.[1] For a variety of reasons this aid never reached the volume of that which flowed across the Atlantic. Still, the United States was heavily involved in the Far East in ways and for reasons which did not obtain in Europe.

The remarkable thing about U.S. commitments in the Far East was that there they brought the nation face to face with an aggressor. Japanese aggression, especially in the East and South China Seas, affected American interests directly. Whether those interests were vital or less than vital, the direct confrontation of the two powers made U.S. involvement inescapable. For many years a regiment of the

---

[1] For a full account of this aid see Charles F. Romanus and Riley Sunderland, Stilwell's Mission to China (Washington: U.S. Government Printing Office, 1953), Chap. i.

U.S. Army was stationed in China as was the U.S. Asiatic Fleet, which included a shore-based garrison of Marines. These forces were present to back up the Open Door Policy as well as to protect American lives and property from bandits. They were clearly too weak to deter a determined violation of the Open Door, however. The army regiment was withdrawn in 1938 and the Marines and the last of the Fleet in November 1941.

Even when the Aisatic Fleet withdrew, it went only as far as Manila. There in the Philippines, still a part of the Far East, the nation was far more heavily involved than in any other place outside the Western Hemisphere. It was responsible for the defense of the islands and repeatedly affirmed its intent to defend them. Military planners, however, had long recognized the infeasibility of their defense with the military forces available. The Japanese reached the same conclusion.

Without sufficient military strength to defend against an invading force, the United States depended upon two principle deterrents to any such plans on the part of the Japanese. For one thing, economic sanctions were imposed, not only by the United States, but in lesser degrees by the Dutch and British as well. This failed to deter Japan from further aggression and may well have had an opposite effect from that intended. Japan was so committed to operations on the mainland, where she was expending great amounts of munitions and supplies, that the reduction and threatened further reduction of imports of petroleum and other raw materials created for her a desperate need to seize the sources of these materials by force. This deterrent measure was thus more harmful than helpful.

The second great deterrent was the U.S. Pacific Fleet. It could not physically prevent further expansion by Japan nor regain territory once lost, but it was a powerful and growing force, and it could wreak a fearful vengeance upon Japan's Navy and her sea commerce. This deterrent failed too. More than that, its very existence invited attack. It can never be known for certain whether the United States would have intervened if Japan had confined her December attack to Dutch and British areas, but the Pacific Fleet would have constituted so serious a threat to the flank of such operations to the south that the Japanese felt compelled to make their first strike against it. The Far East Air Force in the Philippines was growing at such a rate that it was becoming a similar threat. The same reasoning by the Japanese compelled them to destroy that threat also in their initial operations.

Thus, two of the principal deterrents, the first (economic sanctions) virtually assured a movement south by the Japanese (although in large part this was simply used as an excuse by the militarists) and the second (threat of military retaliation) virtually assured that the United States would be involved in the war from the start.

The military planners had long recognized that the immediate threat to American interests was in the Pacific and not against the more vulnerable Atlantic flank. It was simply the current state of international relations which accounts for their long preoccupation with the Pacific and with problems of a war with Japan. As the power and aggressiveness of the European Axis Powers grew in the middle and late 1930's, the French Army and the British Navy stood between them and America. No one stood between America and Japan. And the increasing attention the planners paid to the Atlantic during 1940 and 1941 resulted not from any change in basic strategic concepts but from a need for American military power to counter-balance the scales as they tipped more and more in favor of the Axis <u>vis-a-vis</u> the European democracies.

This prewar strategic planning, the length of its history, and its comprehensiveness, was unique in American experience. It succeeded quite well, if less than perfectly, in coordinating itself with national policy and with the involvements and commitments of the nation beyond its shores. On occasion it even anticipated national policy. Whatever measure of success it did achieve may be credited almost solely to the leaders and to the strategic planners of the Army and the Navy. Until 1938 strategic planning was conducted with a minimum of coordination with the non-military departments of the government, with little guidance from the President or his Secretary of State, and with little sympathy and support from the Congress. The penalty for this lack of coordination was not a lack of plans, but there were penalties, nevertheless. One was the unfortunate subordination of the Department of State and the submersion of long-range political aims to the imperatives of military strategy and operations during the war very much as the influence of the service departments were suppressed and the needs of defense were neglected in time of peace. Without a healthy tradition of coordination of state policy and military planning in peacetime, it was even more difficult to coordinate the two in time of war. During the war military needs were supreme and there was no substitute for nor any higher objective than military victory -- this despite occasional protests to the contrary.

A second penalty was a poor state of physical preparedness before the war. Military armament was poorly coordinated with political commitments and with strategic planning, lagging far behind both. Nevertheless, a modest build-up did begin in 1938 and continued thereafter at a gradually accelerated rate. It had proceeded so far that only six months of disaster and retreat followed the start of the war, ending at Midway. It had come so far that in less than a year the United States was able to mount modest counteroffensives in both the Pacific and Atlantic theaters.[1] The country had not been so well prepared for any of its other major wars. The direct predictions by military officers that next time there would not be enough time to mobilize after the war began did not come true.[2] The nation was at least partially mobilized, and although tragedy followed, national disaster did not. One more time, after all, the nation profited immensely from the existence of two wide moats and of fighting allies.

---

[1] On Guadalcanal in August 1942, against Buna in New Guinea the next month, and, two months later, in North Africa.

[2] See, e.g., the W.D. 1929 *Survey*, p. 20.

An important part of the rearmament program was the assistance given to the enemies of the Axis Powers. The value of this policy was two-fold: it helped arm the future allies, sustaining them until the United States was better prepared to fight, and it assisted considerably in the massive and complex task of industrial mobilization.

Closely akin to the program of aid to the allies was the conduct of coalition planning with the United Kingdom and other members of the Commonwealth. This was a great spur to the coordination of national policy, strategy, and rearmament. In fact, the activity was at once an example of foreign policy in action, of strategic planning, and, in a sense, of rearmament. This last is true to the extent that the coordination of strategy affected an accretion to the military strength of both nations.

Wartime Planning and Operations

The basic strategy for prosecuting a global war and the basic strategy to be employed in the Pacific Theater were agreed upon by Britain and the United States before Pearl Harbor. The first, the Europe-first strategy, was formally reconfirmed at each wartime strategy conference; but commitment of forces to other theaters of operations, especially to the Pacific, dissipated Allied strength far more than the planners had expected and thereby weakened the main effort in Europe. The original strategy in the Pacific for making the main effort through the Mandates was modified even more. So much of the momentum of the Pacific offensive was directed along the New Guinea-Philippines route of advance that the actual movement of the bulk of the Navy across the Central Pacific hardly proves the contention often made that the war itself moved via that route.

In the context of global strategy the Allies fought a defensive war in the Pacific until very near the end. But to describe Allied strategy in the Pacific as defensive, even strategically defensive, can be seriously misleading. The counteroffensive which began in the late summer of 1942 was extended during the next year to other areas of the Pacific as well as to Southeast Asia and China. It gathered momentum markedly and continually during the last two years of the war and reached a fury of intensity in air, sea,, and land battles long before the atomic bomb burst over Hiroshima. In fact, the phases of the war against Japan paralleled those against Germany and Italy quite closely.

Nevertheless, the Europe-first strategy was never successfully challenged during the war. Many reasons have already been presented and some will be discussed tangentially below for this near paradox of an unwavering commitment to a Europe-first strategy and an almost equal expenditure of effort in the Pacific. One explanation of this is simply that a strategy or a course of action, once a significant commitment has been made to it, begins to generate its own imperatives; the very pursuance of it is a self-reenforcing argument for continuing it. Thus it was that the commitment to an Atlantic (Europe)-first strategy long before the war began had a great deal to do with continuing the strategy during periods of altered circumstances when, theoretically at least, better arguments could have been brought forth in favor of changing it to a Pacific-first strategy. Yet, despite this firm commitment, there were immediate and ineluctable pressures to send reinforcements first to the Pacific and even to undertake the first counteroffensive there. After that it was often more difficult tp give real meaning to the Europe-first strategy than it was to maintain simply a verbal commitment to it.

There were times when the planners, Army and Navy, American and British, argued for the Europe-first strategy for wrong reasons. Repeatedly they stated that since Germany was the leading member of the Axis Powers, the major military effort of the United States should be made in the Atlantic.[1] The strategy itself was sound in the circumstances; it suited the situation admirably but for reasons rarely if ever properly stated. Even with Germany remaining the strongest and the leading member of the Axis Powers, two entirely different sets of circumstances might have existed in which it would clearly not have been wise for the United States to concentrate in the Atlantic. The first would have existed if the European Allies had been defeated, the second if they had been strong enough to stand without substantial American assistance. In the first circumstance the United States could not have defeated the European Axis, certainly not unless she had first made her Pacific flank perfectly safe, thereby allowing a total concentration of her military strength against Germany and Italy. In that case it may have been both possible and wise to defend the Atlantic flank with minimum strength while concentrating first on Japan.

---

[1] See, e.g., ABC-1.

In the second circumstance it may have been best to allow the European Allies to take care of Germany and Italy while the United States concentrated on Japan, thereby greatly shortening the war.

The condition which actually existed was just half way between these two. The Allies were not strong enough to take care of Germany by themselves, but there was a good chance that American help would save them. Even under these conditions a strong case could be made for the wisdom of supporting Britain and Russia barely sufficiently to prevent their collapse and then concentrating American (and some Allied) strength for an early victory over Japan. The most vulnerable point in such a strategy would be its dependence on the precision needed in fixing the limit of aid. The danger attending a miscalculation would demand that a comfortable margin of aid first be extended to Britain and Russia. Having extended this margin (as was actually the case by the middle of 1943) the most efficient course would be to continue the concentration in Europe until victory was achieved. A better justification for the Europe-first strategy, therefore, would have been on the basis not simply that Germany was the strongest enemy but that, in the first instance, there was more to be saved in Europe. Loss of the whole vast Pacific, tragic as that would have been, would not have been so disastrous to the ultimate cause of the Allies as the loss of the island of Great Britain and of European Russia. It would be foolish to claim that the military leaders did not realize all this perfectly well. In one way or another they expressed these same ideas from time to time. But failure to express them clearly and succinctly as the reason for the Europe-first strategy led sometimes to their arguing from spurious premises.

In a somewhat similar fashion the accepted strategy within the Pacific was never perfectly aligned with the deployment of forces. An advance across the Central Pacific was the strategy of both ORANGE and RAINBOW planning. The concept had joint Army and Navy approval, but many Army officers had serious reservations about some aspects of it. It enjoyed a more wholehearted acceptance by the Navy. Besides the planners in Washington, every student at the Naval War College studied the plan in detail and war gamed it there and while serving with the Fleet in the Pacific. This familiarity with the concept and their great confidence in its soundness were strong reasons for naval officers to be inclined to follow it when war came, fitting the circumstances to the plan when necessary. Navy spokesmen after the war habitually averred that this was the strategy actually followed in the Pacific War. But the first reinforcements were not sent to the Central Pacific bases west of Hawaii but to the Philippines and the lines of communications to them from the South Pacific. Finally, the first counteroffensive was undertaken from the South Pacific. After that, although there were many reasons offered for continuing a strong effort along this route of advance, each operation, each success, and each increment of strength added to the South and Southwest Pacific forces the most effective arguments for a further concentration of effort there. A good case was finally developed for an advance along both routes, and the case was not impaired by the fact that it had been impossible to get agreement to concentration on just one of the two routes anyway.

Service Differences Over Strategy

Disagreement over the proper route of advance in the Pacific, like other disagreements over strategy, was largely an inter-service dispute. The strategy debates were conducted by skilled professional officers who were earnestly seeking the most objectively logical solutions to their problems. They succeeded admirably, but it was unavoidable that each officer should bring to his task certain preconcoptions of warfare which were typical of the service he represented. The greatest heat was generated when the opposing solutions offered would clearly have an effect on personal or service prestige or on the postwar relationships of the services. Even so, these differences should not be dismissed simply as parochial and petty bickering. The protagonists were men of intelligence and professional competence, men with a high sense of honor and of public responsibility. Behind their concern for personal prestige was a concern for service prestige; behind that was a concern for the long-run position of the services to each other and to the society they served; and behind this were deep-seated convictions about the safety of the nation. No doubt less noble motives intruded themselves from time to time into the debates on strategy, but this is to admit nothing more than that the strategists were human beings.

Virtually all of the service differences, including those concerning such seemingly disparate problems as the interpretation of offense and defense, the routes of advance, the selection of commanders, and the requirements of the unconditional surrender policy sprang from the same source — the difference in the instruments at the disposal of army and of navy commanders. The nature of those instruments was different as was the relative quantity of them available to the two services.

A good example of this influence is the curious fact that the words "defense" and "offense" do not mean the same thing to naval officers that they do to army officers. This difference begins at the tactical level and is carried over to create divergent views and concepts at the strategic level as well. Tactically, there is virtually no difference between defensive and offensive operations in naval warfare. A combatant ship is at once almost equally a defensive and an offensive weapon and its actions in either situation is very nearly the same. This is so because of its mobility; it draws both offensive and defensive power from its ability to move and to shoot while moving. Moreover, the effectiveness of its protective fires are unimpaired while moving, and it carries its protective armor with it. A static defense in open seas simply makes no sense to the Navy, which resists having to maintain even an area defense. Only occasionally is immobility deliberately employed as a means of concealment. Submarines can use this tactic at any time and surface ships can use it during periods of low visibility.

For the Army, on the other hand, there has traditionally been a distinct difference between defense and offense. The defensive power of an army unit can be greatly increased through the proper utilization of terrain and by defense from fixed positions. It has always been most vulnerable when maneuvering in the face of the enemy. But the more mobile the army unit the less difference there is between the offensive and defensive tactics it employs. For this reason a cavalryman of past years could perhaps better appreciate naval tactics than could other army officers. In more recent years the tactics of highly mobile forces, especially in flat or rolling desert and prairie areas, resemble even more the tactics of naval warfare than did the tactics of horse cavalry. In passing, it may be remarked that with instruments of an advancing technology coming into its hands the Army is adjusting its tactics and techniques to enable it to "move, shoot, and communicate" over any terrain. The desirability of this adjustment exists independent of the great need of it to meet the requirements of the atomic battlefield.

These different views of offensive and defensive operations partially explain the Army's objection before the war to what it considered the premature offensive operations planned by the Navy. The Navy, on the other hand, considered the Army's plan for defense as disastrously passive. Notwithstanding these differences the Army agreed with the Navy that decisive results could be achieved only by offensive actions. Defensive measures were employed on the battlefield only when necessary because of inferior strength or to economize on strength in one area in order to concentrate offensive strength in another. But in the prewar era only the Navy had forces in being strong enough for offensive operations.

After the war began, the service disagreements over strategy were of a different sort, although they were still rooted in the same ground. Before Pearl Harbor the Army seemed ultra-conservative and concerned primarily with problems of defense while the Navy insisted on planning for an early offensive in the Pacific. But after the war was underway the position of the two services was in some ways reversed. Then it was the Army who was impatient of the strategies which would prolong the war even though they held promise of being cheaper. Neither service had originated the unconditional surrender policy, but the Army accepted and adjusted more readily to the total war strategy which it entailed. A total war strategy was simply not compatible with naval warfare. Naval forces could attack the enemy's navy and sea commerce and thereby reduce both his will and his means of resistance. These attacks on an island nation such as Japan could be profound indeed, but whether they could so strengthen the very existence of the nation as to cause it to surrender unconditionally was doubtful. Naval forces alone could almost totally destroy the offensive capability of such an enemy nation and could even deprive it of some of its overseas conquests. What a Navy could do was to overcome totally the defensive power of such a nation.

Although aerial and naval warfare had many common characteristics, the former was much more compatible with a strategy of total war. For one thing air forces could reach deep into the enemy homeland, where its attacks affected immediately and directly the will of the enemy population in a way impossible for naval forces and even impossible for army forces except in the final stages of an offensive. On the other hand air forces could not destroy in so direct a manner as could naval forces the offensive and expansionist capabilities of an island nation. Their attacks on this capability were partly direct (on its sea communications and on naval and other military forces) but mainly indirect (on the internal communications, on morale, on the industrial complex, and on military installations). Yet this indirect attack on his offensive power could, theoretically, totally destroy the enemy and, thus, totally destroy both his offensive and defensive capability. In its ultimate form, therefore, offensive and defensive warfare was the same to the Air Forces. Tactically, too, when opposing air forces are contesting for supremacy, there is little between the offense and defense. In this case, as in naval warfare, the reason is the great mobility of the airplane.

The Army took more readily than did either the Navy or the Air Forces to the consequences of the unconditional surrender policy. Like the Air Forces, it could literally destroy the enemy, but it was not so inhibited by the moral restraints opposing such drastic action, for it had other means of forcing unconditional surrender on an enemy. Only army forces could seize the enemy (citizens, territory, and governmental machinery) without destroying him and could thereby prevent his further resistance even though his will to do so persisted. This ability became more than merely theoretical as U.S. military forces of all the services burgeoned to great strength by mid-war.

The Winning Strategy

Which strategy, then, was actually pursued in the Pacific? Can one theater, one service or one concept be credited for bringing about the defeat of Japan? Can one of them even be given the most credit? Conflicting claims have been made.

According to Admiral King and Walter M. Whitehall:

> Upon Marshall's insistence, which also reflected MacArthur's views, the Joint Chiefs had prepared plans for landing in Kyushu and eventually in the Toyko plain. King and Leahy did not like the idea, but as unanimpus decisions were necessary in the Joint Chief meetings, they reluctantly acquiesced, feeling that in the end sea power would accomplish the defeat of Japan, as proved to be the case.[1]

According to Admiral Leahy:

> The agreement on fundamental strategy to be employed in defeating Japan and the President's familiarity with the situation acquired at /the July 1944/ conference /in Hawaii/ were to be of great value in preventing an unnecessary invasion of Japan which the planning staffs of the Joint Chiefs and the War Department were advocating, regardless of the loss of life that would result from an attack on Japan's ground forces in their own country. MacArthur and Nimitz were now in agreement that the Philippines should be recovered with ground and air power then available in the western Pacific and that Japan could be forced to accept our terms of surrender by the use of sea and air power without an invasion of the Japanese homeland.[2]

Admiral Leahy managed to crowd a great deal of error into one brief paragraph. For one thing, it is difficult to see what the President's knowledge gained at the conference had to do with the Japanese decision

---

[1] Fleet Admiral Ernest J. King and Walter Muir Whitehall, *Fleet Admiral King* (New York: Norton Co., 1952), p. 598.

[2] Fleet Admiral William D. Leahy, *I Was There* (New York: McGraw-Hill Book Co., 1950), p. 251.

to surrender before the invasion took place. For another, it is simply not true that MacArthur believed that sea and air power were sufficient to force Japan to surrender. In addition, Leahy seems to say that those who were convinced that invasion was necessary lacked both wit and a sense of responsibility. This is a patently unjust charge.

Air Force spokesmen have generally made more cautious claims for air power. General Arnold told his colleagues in the JCS shortly before the first atomic bomb was used against Japan that increased air operations "might cause a capitulation of the enemy, and, in any event, will assure the success of the land campaign in Japan, and reduce the loss of American lives to a minimum." He later reflected that "the surrender of Japan was not entirely the result of the two atomic bombs" and cited approvingly the "many Japanese leaders who gave credit to the Superfortress attacks on interior Japan and Japanese industrial cities as the greatest single factor in forcing their surrender."[1]

Professors Craven and Cate, editors of the multi-volume history of the Army Air Forces in World War II, conclude that both sea and air power should be credited for the victory. They find some difficulty in apportioning the credit between the two but state confidently that the role of the Army was a subordinate and supporting one. Somehow they seem to have found proof that the Army's invasion concept

---

[1] H. H. Arnold, *Global Mission* (New York: Harper and Brothers, 1949), pp. 596, 598.

was at least professionally if not morally wrong. By the spring of 1945, they said,

> certain individuals in Washington, particularly Acting Secretary of State Joseph C. Grew and Secretary of War Henry L. Stimson, correctly diagnosed the situation in Japan and thought that the nation might be brought to surrender without an invasion if an increasing show of force could be accompanied by a public statement that the Allied demand for unconditional surrender did not contemplate the destruction of the Emperor or of the Japanese nation. Others, impressed with the fanatical resistance of the Japanese at Iwo Jima and Okinawa and aware of the existence in Japan of a large and undefeated army, believed that an invasion in force would be necessary. If these latter leaders failed to appreciate conditions familiar to us all through postwar disclosures, it must be remembered in their favor that they were committed to winding up the war as soon as possible and that preparations for so large an invasion demanded an early decision on strategy.[1]

The last sentence is a gratuitous and unnecessary apology for "these latter leaders." Moreover, in light of the many statements of Mr. Grew that the Japanese were likely to fight to the bitter end unless an offer of peace terms considerably short of unconditional surrender were offered, it does not seem likely that Messrs Craven and Cate have correctly stated Grew's position.

The civilian directors of the Strategic Bombing Survey refused to claim that any one of several causes contributed most to Japan's defeat. They concluded "that certainly prior to 31 December 1945, and in all probability prior to 1 November 1945, Japan would have surrendered even if the atomic bombs had not been dropped, even if

---

[1] Wesley Frank Craven and James Lea Cate, eds, *The Pacific: Matterhorn to Nagasaki, June 1944 to August 1945* (Chicago: The University of Chicago Press, 1953), pp. xxii - xxiii, 736 - 37.

Russia had not entered the war, and even if no invasion had been planned or contemplated."[1]

No well articulated claim has been made for the decisive nature of land power in bringing Japan to defeat except by the Russians. In their book not only was it land power but specifically the Soviet land offensive in Manchuria which defeated Japan. The preceding chapters have not laid the ground work for making bold claims for the decisiveness of land power, but a few comments can be made which may restore a more balanced view.

Every stepping stone which Allied forces gained as they moved ever nearer Japan were looked upon differently by supporters of the different strategies. The Navy looked upon each as one step in the projection of naval power westward, one more tightening of the noose about the neck of Japan. The Air Forces, especially in the latter stages of the war, looked upon each as a base from which long-range bombardment could be conducted. The Army looked upon each as one step nearer, first, the recovery of the Philippines and, finally, the invasion of Japan. These were the primary considerations. Each service recognized a certain legitimacy in the views of others. Also, each recognized the defensive value of every step forward in depriving the enemy of advance bases and in destroying enemy forces.

The advance of land power was doing more than this, however. In the Philippines, in Southeast Asia, in the Indies, in China, in

---

[1] *Summary Report (Pacific War)*, p. 26.

Manchuria, and in Korea it was depriving Japan of her empire and of all that she was fighting the war for. Moreover, despite the conclusion of the Strategic Bombing Survey, it cannot be demonstrated that if the Allies had not clearly had the means, the plans, <u>and the intent</u> to invade, Japan would still have surrendered when she did.

In any case the use of the atomic bomb, which was the proximate cause of Japan's surrender, cannot properly be considered an application of air power, of sea power, or of land power. In the strictest sense it was not the possession and use of the atomic bomb, anyway, which precipitated the Japanese surrender; rather it was the <u>exclusive</u> possession and use of it. The experience, therefore, has little relevance in a situation of a lost monopoly of the bomb.

In retrospect it would be difficult to imagine a more thorough integration of land, sea, and air forces than that which carried Allied forces forward from Australia and Hawaii. Even if the invasion had proved necessary, the defeat of Japan could not properly have been ascribed simply to land power any more than it should now be ascribed to sea power or air power. Nor should any fault be found with the decision to invade and with the preparations for it. What might be criticized is the demand for unconditional surrender. For a number of reasons it was an even less appropriate policy toward Japan than toward Germany. Naval power, generously supported by land and sea forces, could have forced Japan's agreement to a reasonable peace settlement. This, however, would not only have greatly postponed the liberation of the Philippines but would also have involved imposing a cruel blockade on those wards and friends of the United States. And unless the peace terms offered Japan were extremely liberal, the United States may still have had to build up an invasion force strong enough to constitute a credible threat of invasion. Lastly, one might speculate and reach unhappy conclusions about the vulnerability to invasion and subversion by Russia of a Japan weakened by a naval defeat and a long, tight blockade.

Even Admiral King, that most convinced of believers in the decisiveness of naval power in the Pacific War, gave generous credit to the blending of opposing service views which took place within the organization of the Joint Chiefs of Staff. He claimed that

> when the history of the Joint Chiefs of Staff comes to be written, their record will show how many proposals -- including some of my own -- had to yield to cogent reasoning of one or more members.
>
> During the last war, in over-all strategic guidance, the proposals or convictions of no one member of the Joint Chiefs of Staff were as sound or as promising of success as the united judgement and agreed decisions of the group. [1]

There have been some more or less subtle suggestions in this summation of lessons from the World War II experience which have some application to the problems of strategic planning in the age of guided missiles and nuclear weapons. It does not seem appropriate at this point to go beyond those simple suggestions. Newspaper headlines at the end of the war, just as at the end of World War I, proclaimed that America had finally learned her lesson. For the most part these

---

[1] King and Whitehead, *Fleet Admiral King*, p. 645.

proclamations were referring to the need for maintaining adequate defenses. But profiting from an experience requires more than a will to do so; it requires also the wisdom properly to assess the experience and to draw from it the real and not merely the superficially apparent lessons.

One lesson which seemingly was learned anew was that war is not something apart from politics but is itself a political art. It follows that all war activities are political. Few people would quarrel with this statement today. The 1950's were a decade of much intellectual interest in and of scholarly investigation of the relationship of military objectives and national policy (often treated under the inappropriate title of civil-military relations). Yet the ready agreement with the statement may be a hollow one. There is still a strong tendency to separate sharply the civil (erroneously equated to "political") from the military, peace from war. There continues a widespread refusal to recognize the many subtle gradations between total war and total peace. Even the political realists, who are keenly aware of the role of force in international politics, are usually interested only in politics short of war; the politics of war is, to date, a phrase virtually devoid of meaning.

The current status of the U.S. military establishment and the current national strategy is a reflection of the American public's continued disposition to make this sharp distinction between war and no war. Weapon technology has changed; the significance of time and space has changed; but, just as before World War II, the peacetime military establishment (including no doubt, the strategic plans) is still designed more to deter a war than to prosecute one successfully if it should come despite the deterrence. There is still a dangerous tendency to overemphasize a strategy of massive deterrence; but who is thinking about how victory will be achieved if deterrence fails? More important, who can say what the nation's aspirations are beyond military victory; or, perhaps more accurately, what will constitute, what will the nation accept as victory? The answer to this question should precede all preparations for victory, but if it exists, it has not been well or publicly articulated. The nation has learned many lessons about the use of military force in time of peace and about the use of non-violent means and of carefully controlled violence in time of war but not nearly so much as is popularly supposed.

APPENDIX A

Chronology of Some Important Combat Actions and Events of the War in the Pacific [1]

1941

7 Dec (8 Dec Philippine time) - Pearl Harbor attack; attack on Clark Field; landings on Batan I. (150 mi. no. of Luzon); striking force of Asiatic Fleet departs Phil. I. for N.E. I; gunboat Wake surrenders at Shanghai; U.S. Marines and nationals interned at Shanghai and Tientsin; landings in Malaya; invasion of Thailand.

10 Dec - Guam surrenders.

22 Dec - Luzon and Borneo invaded.

23 Dec - Wake surrenders.

25 Dec - Hong Kong surrenders.

1942

2 Jan - Manila occupied.

7 Jan - Siege of Bataan begins.

11 Jan - Invasion of N.E.I. begins.

15 Jan-25 Feb - Period of ABDACOM.

1 Feb - U.S. Pacific Fleet attacks Roi, Kwajalein, Wotje, Tarao, Jaluit, and Makin Islands in the Marshalls and Gilberts.

2 Feb - Gen. Stilwell appointed Chief of Staff to the Supreme Commander, China Theater.

15 Feb - Singapore surrenders.

22 Feb - President orders MacArthur to Australia.

---

[1] All dates based on those listed in Mary Williams, *Chronology, 1941-1945* (Washington: U.S. Government Printing Office, 1960); and Navy Department, *Naval Chronology, World War II* (Washington: U.S. Government Printing Office, 1955).

9 Mar - Java fails.

11-17 Mar - MacArthur en route to Mindanao and Australia.

30 Mar - First directives to MacArthur as CINCSWPA and to Nimitz as CINCPOA; Japanese occupy Christmas Island.

9 Apr - Luzon Force surrenders.

27 Apr - Doolittle raid on Tokyo; Battle of Java Sea.

4-8 May - Battle of Coral Sea.

6 May - Corregidor fails.

4-6 Jun - Battle of Midway.

7 Jun - Attu and Kiska seized.

22 Jun - Submarine shells Ft. Stevens, Ore.

7 Aug - Invasion of Guadalcanal begins; Battle of Savo I.

25 Aug - Australians begin counter-offensive from Port Moresby toward Kokoda Pass (and, later, on toward Buna-Gona area).

6 Nov - Advance echelon of GHQ, SWPA established in New Guinea at Port Moresby.

9 Dec - Gona captured.

14 Dec - Buna captured.

1943

22 Jan - Papua campaign ends.

9 Feb - Resistance ceases on Guadalcanal.

21 Feb - Unopposed landing in Russell Islands.

2-5 Mar - Battle of the Bismark Sea.

18 Apr - Adm. Yamamoto killed when his plane shot down.

11-30 May - Attu recaptured.

30 Jun - CARTWHEEL begins with landings in central Solomons (New Georgia, Rendova, and others) in the Trobriands (Woodlark, and Kiriwina), and in New Guinea (Nassau Bay).

6 Aug - Battle of Vella Gulf.

15 Aug - Unopposed landing on Kiska.

4 Sep - Landing in Lae, beginning operations to seize Huon Gulf area.

27 Oct - Landings in Treasury Islands, beginning operations for northern Solomons.

1 Nov - Landing on Bougainville (on Empress Augusta Bay).

2 Nov - Battle of Empress Augusta Bay.

15 Dec - Invasion of Western New Britain.

1944

2 Jan - Landing at Saidor.

31 Jan-7 Feb - Kwajalein invaded.

15 Feb - Green Islands invaded.

17 Feb - Eniwetok invaded.

29 Feb-18 May - Reconnaissance in Force of the Admiralties (Los Negros).

20 Mar - Unopposed invasion of St. Matthias Islands (Emirau).

22 Apr - Landings at Aitape and Hollandia.

17 May - Wadke Island invaded.

27 May - Biak Island invaded.

15 Jun - Saipan invaded.

19-20 Jun - Battle of the Philippine Sea.

6 Jul - Noemfoor seized.

21 Jul - Guam invaded.

24 Jul - Tinian invaded.

30 Jul - The Vogelkop invaded (vicinity of Sansapor).

15 Sep - Morotai and Peliliu invaded.

22 Sep - Ulithi invaded.

20 Oct - Leyte invaded.

23-26 Oct - Battle for Leyte Gulf (including Battle of Surigao Strait, 25 Oct).

15 Dec - Mindora invaded.

1945

9 Jan - Luzon invaded.

19 Feb - Iwo Jima invaded.

28 Feb - Palawan invaded.

10 Mar - Mindanao invaded.

26 Mar - Ryukyu operations begin with landings on Kerami Island.

1 Apr - Okinawa invaded.

1 May - Tarakan Island (off Borneo) invaded.

6 May - Reorganization of Pacific: MacArthur commands all Army Forces and Nimitz all Naval Forces.

10 Jun - Borneo (Burnei Bay) invaded.

1 Jul - Balikpapan (Borneo) landing.

13 Jul - Italy declared war on Japan.

16 Jul - First atomic bomb test.

26 Jul - Potsdam Declaration calling for Japan's unconditional surrender.

6 Aug - Atomic bomb dropped on Hiroshima.

9 Aug - Atomic bomb dropped on Nagasaki; Russia declares war on Japan.

14 Aug - Japan accepts provision of Potsdam Declaration.

2 Sep - Surrender documents signed.

www.ingramcontent.com/pod-product-compliance
Lightning Source LLC
Chambersburg PA
CBHW081836170426
43199CB00017B/2744